inform

...ase return on or before the last
...d below.

...owdery

Copywriting

n. the creative process
of writing text for
advertisements or
publicity material

An AVA Book

Published by AVA Publishing SA
Rue des Fontenailles 16
Case Postale
1000 Lausanne 6
Switzerland

Tel: +41 786 005 109
Email: enquiries@avabooks.ch

Distributed by Thames & Hudson (ex-North America)
181a High Holborn
London WC1V 7QX
United Kingdom

Tel: +44 20 7845 5000
Fax: +44 20 7845 5055
Email: sales@thameshudson.co.uk
www.thamesandhudson.com

Distributed in the USA & Canada by:
Watson-Guptill Publications
770 Broadway
New York, New York 10003
USA

Fax: +1 646 654 5487
Email: info@watsonguptill.com
www.watsonguptill.com

English Language Support Office
AVA Publishing (UK) Ltd.

Tel: +44 1903 204 455
Email: enquiries@avabooks.co.uk

ISBN 2-940373-68-X and 978-2-940373-68-0

10 9 8 7 6 5 4 3 2 1

Design by David Shaw

Production by
AVA Book Production Pte. Ltd., Singapore

Tel: +65 6334 8173
Fax: +65 6259 9830
Email: production@avabooks.com.sg

Contents

This book aims to provide you with a detailed introduction to the art and craft of copywriting. Instead of just offering a theoretical approach, I'm going to be showing you some examples of good advertising and analysing how and why the ideas and text in these ads work so well.

In addition to traditional forms of print advertising, such as billboards, press ads and mail packs, I'll be reviewing selected TV and radio advertising and looking at modern media communications such as websites and ambient advertising.

There will be practical pointers along the way, providing you with tips and techniques that can help improve your writing skills – and boost your powers of persuasion.

And to get you thinking and working harder, I'm going to include some creative writing exercises where you can develop your conceptual cleverness and sharpen your verbal dexterity.

Adopting the right tone of voice

56 ⊳ 57

Knowing your audience

Having established who your audience are, and what is most likely to appeal to them, you now need to decide how you're going to talk to them.

When it comes to writing adverts, the best copywriters are chameleon-like in their ability to adopt a different persona, but how different is that from how we all tend to act in front of different audiences?

Would you use the same tone of voice and choice of language when talking to these various people: your close friends, your partner, your parents, your boss, your bank manager, the policeman who's stopped you for speeding, the magistrate who's about to hand down your sentence?

Your tone of voice and use of language depends on your audience and that can vary considerably in terms of the type and level of language they understand, as well as the impression you're trying to make.

It's sometimes helpful to think about the tone of voice used by different newspapers whose journalists adjust their style to appeal to their different readerships. Try and think of the tone and style adopted by The Sun versus The Times, or The Daily Mail versus The Guardian, etc.

Then consider how journalists would write up the same story for those different newspapers. Here's a sample of what I mean, where I've taken a typical summer heatwave story but written it up in two very different styles. Can you tell the subtle difference?

Hottest July since records began
The meteorological office reports that July has been the hottest on record with a mean temperature of 24 degrees Celsius (75 degrees Fahrenheit). There have been government warnings of hosepipe bans coming into force at the end of August unless significant rain falls in the next two weeks.

Stunning Suzy sizzles in the sun
Phwoar – it's enough to get anyone hot under the collar. Temperatures soared this month and it's no wonder as sultry Suzy and her sexy chums got down to the bare essentials and frolicked in the sea at Southend. If this is global warming, well, we say bring it on – and let's get 'em off.

Obviously, my first journalistic treatment was modelled on The Times while the second was cleverly modified for The Church Times.

Right:
There are many newspapers out there and they're targeted at different audiences. It can help you create the right tone of voice for your advertising by thinking about such journalistic styles.

Now it's your turn

Try taking a story from a 'serious' newspaper and rewriting it in the style of a more popular 'red-top' daily. It should be possible to have some fun with this exercise.

How can you make the story more immediate, punchier, snappier? What kind of headline will you use? How do you get the main points of the story across without losing dramatic impact?

Will you choose to emphasise just one aspect of the story? Will you try and seek out the comic possibilities in an otherwise serious report to appeal to a new audience?

Research can help you find out who it is you're meant to be talking to but it's up to you to adjust your tone of voice to try and appeal to that particular audience.

Can you rely on market research? | Adopting the right tone of voice

Headings
Prominent section headings to help you quickly locate a topic of interest.

Images
A wide range of successful adverts and powerful images chosen to illustrate the principles discussed.

Word-check
Useful definitions of key words and advertising phrases.

Speaking an international language

If you do have to write an advert or any other marketing copy that you know will need to be translated into other languages, you must try to avoid complex wordplays and local idioms. Otherwise your work might well get lost in translation.

Even countries whose inhabitants often have an excellent command of the English language can miss aspects of English humour. For example, the actor and comedian, Bill Bailey, tells the story of how a great many Norwegians love the TV comedy he appeared in called *Black Books* which is set in a dysfunctional second-hand bookshop run by eccentric Bernard Black, brilliantly played by Dylan Moran.

However, rather than call the show *Black Books* the Norwegians chose to rename this show in a very obvious and un-English way as, *Crazy Shop*. It appears from such small details that we're not always on the same wavelength. No wonder language needs fine-tuning for different audiences.

And if your text can't be translated easily, then it will probably need to be extensively and expensively adapted by a specialist agency. These adaptation agencies tend to employ advertising copywriters who are capable of taking a basic translation and making it work in their own native language. Frequently the adaptations end up being very different from the original text – and for good reason: many clever concepts with witty words don't translate very well.

Take the example of a French airport which wanted to suggest it was the quickest gateway to the skiing resorts in the French Pyrenees. They required their French advert to be adapted into English. The image showed the front of an airplane with ski tips appearing over the cockpit as if they were being carried in the same way as on the roof of a car.

The French headline: *Dans les Pyrenees, la saison commence sur nos pistes* (In the Pyrenees, the season begins on our runways) relies on the fact that the word 'piste' can mean both an airport runway and a ski run. This pun works well in French but it cannot be translated directly into English. An alternative heading was required if the same image of the plane was going to be used.

The English version the adaptation agency came up with relied on a far weaker wordplay: *Skiing in the Pyrenees. There's a way to jet there faster.* My own version, taking on board the comedy visual of the plane carrying skis, also uses a wordplay but one which I hope has greater humorous impact: *Now there's a quicker way to slope off to the Pyrenees.*

Sometimes you have to be brave and tell your client that the same concept is not going to work as well in another language for another culture. It's time to come up with some fresh ideas.

EXCLUSIVEMENT
réservé aux jeunes
forces vives

SFR

Some ideas don't travel so well

Just to show that even excellent straplines don't always travel well, there's the story concerning Nike's informal yet motivational line *Just do it.* This line worked well for most of the world but apparently not in France where some people supposedly took it the wrong way and complained. 'I'm not going to *do it* and no one is going to tell me to *do it!*' Perhaps they should have changed it for the French market to *Go your own way* or *Do what you want.*

Left:
This effective concept for low-price French mobile phone packages used a comic image of a dishevelled young bloke with the ironic headline 'Exclusivement réservé aux jeunes forces vives' which can be roughly translated as 'Exclusively reserved for dynamic youth' or 'young people with vibrant energy'. Unfortunately these phrases sound awkward in English and yet the original line works extremely well in French. Here's another case where I believe that a different approach would need to be adopted to make this ad work in the UK.

Client: SFR
Agency: Tequila

Word-check

Zeitgeist – there aren't many modern German words that we use in the English language but 'zeitgeist' is a great one and very popular in discussions of marketing as a way of indicating the latest moods and trends. The word translates as 'spirit of the age' (literally 'time-spirit').

Then there's 'schadenfreude' (harm-joy) which is a mean and marvellous term to describe the wicked feeling of pleasure you get from the misfortune of others.

Meanwhile a more pleasant and socially acceptable sensation: that of cosiness and warmth, is suggested by the word 'gemütlicht'. Mmmm nice.

Now it's your turn
Practical exercises to test and enhance your copywriting skills.

Summaries
Succinct thought-provoking commentaries on the main text.

Chapter navigation
Clear navigation to help you find your way around the book.

Captions
Revealing explanations showing how adverts are made to work.

Introduction

does **winter** make you **feel** like this?

Are you ready for a

The role of copywriters

Copywriters are the people employed to supply the text – otherwise known as copy – that accompanies the imagery in advertisements.

But hang on, that's a bit bland. I think I'm underselling our services and that just won't do in a book on advertising where I'm meant to be using all our industry's powerful and persuasive promotional techniques.

So let's try that again.

Copywriters provide an essential element in the creative process. Without their clever way with words, and their ability to originate ideas, there would be no effective advertising.

That sounds a bit more dynamic.

And picture this – it's not enough just to be good with words. The most successful copywriters are individuals who are as comfortable with the visual as the verbal.

That's because, in creating advertising material, we're trying to establish a connection with our various audiences through an influential combination of imagery *and* words.

Advertising is all about communication. It's about getting people to connect with your product or service at some practical or emotional level.

1 Writing with purpose
An introduction to the role of copywriters: how and where they work and why it's important to be able to think both verbally and visually. Our chief role is as communicators of information and ideas but it's also essential that our concepts and text generate emotional responses in the minds of our audience.

2 Understanding your product
What you might be asked to promote could vary from a packet of cereal to an animal charity so it pays to research your product or service in as much detail as possible. Only then can you apply that product knowledge – and select the right details – to create powerful concepts and copy.

3 Knowing your audience
How well do you know your target audience? Will market research help you gain a better understanding? Once you know who you're talking to – and what you want these people to take away from your advert – you'll be able to adopt the appropriate tone of voice and convey stronger messages.

4 Mastering the language
Language lies at the heart of copywriting so it's a good idea to improve your skills by reading widely. You can also take advantage of various forms of practical and technical assistance. It certainly helps if you know the basic rules of writing – and when it's appropriate to bend or break them.

5 Sharpening your style
A range of tried and tested techniques designed to help you develop a more persuasive writing style and organise your material in more effective ways. You'll also find some valuable tips on how to generate creative ideas and how to use different types of humour to make your ads more memorable.

6 Rules and restrictions
There was a time when advertising was free to tell bare-faced lies, whereas now we're encouraged by the Advertising Standards Authority to be more honest – or risk our ads being pulled. However, there are still some campaigns that actively seek to shock or offend.

7 Creating effective copy
An investigation into creativity and originality with practical examples from selected advertising teams whose work exhibits all the signs of clever lateral thinking. However, don't forget that a direct and straightforward approach sometimes proves to be the most persuasive creative response to an advertising brief.

8 Advertising around the world
English might be considered a world language but you need to be aware of the problems you're bound to face when you write for foreign markets. Concepts can get lost in translation, with unintended comic effects and unhappy marketing consequences.

How to get the most out of this book △ Introduction △ Writing with purpose

There's an enormous range of advertising material that requires creative input from copywriters. It's the sheer variety that makes it so fascinating.

Copywriters are involved in the creation of many different forms of advertising and promotional material – far more than you may at first realise. That's because, when we talk about advertising, we tend to think only of the most high-profile campaigns for established brands: those adverts we see broadcast on mainstream television or pasted onto large billboards.

However, these well-known examples represent only the tip of the proverbial iceberg. In addition to TV ads, billboard posters and adverts in the national press, there are many other types of media where you'll find advertising. For example, over the past few decades, there's been an enormous growth in direct marketing in all its forms, including direct mail.

There's also been the rapid rise of new digital media such as Internet advertising, e-mailing and viral campaigns. And that's without considering the incredible amount of sales and promotional literature that is generated to promote organisations' products or services.

Copywriters are required to work on all these different types of promotional messaging. For example, a copywriter might be asked to write the text for a product pack that will be placed on a supermarket's shelves, a floor vinyl designed to appear in that shop's aisles, a point-of-sale leaflet for customers to pick up from the check-outs, a landing page for their website and even an annual report for that same store. Although preferably not all on the same day.

Left:
Information overload?
Every day we're bombarded
with a massive amount of
advertising. How do we make
our messages stand out?

It's not just within advertising agencies that you'll find copywriters. The skills of the copywriter are also engaged in many other locations where they are used to create ideas and text for a wide variety of promotional and marketing material.

Copywriters are indeed often employed at advertising agencies but they can also be found within direct marketing companies, design consultancies and PR agencies. And that's just on the agency side of operations. Some copywriters work directly for client companies, particularly within the marketing communication departments of medium-sized and larger organisations.

Indeed, many larger companies will have their own in-house creative or design departments, sometimes dealing with day-to-day print and publicity requirements but often actively engaged in full-scale advertising campaigns.

Advertising carries many messages to a great number of different people. It's an essential part of the professional copywriter's job to make sure those messages are delivered successfully.

Depending on the volume of writing required, advertising agencies, design consultancies and other such organisations will either employ full-time copywriters or, if there is only occasional need for writing input, they might hire in freelance copywriters.

As long as they are available, freelance copywriters can be pulled in to work on a particular account (an 'account' is how each client company is described within an agency) and perhaps fill in for a full-time employee who is on holiday, or otherwise deal with a temporary overload of work.

In many ways it makes commercial sense to employ freelance designers and copywriters. An agency or company doesn't want to have these so-called creatives on their full-time payroll if there isn't sufficient work for them to do on a regular basis. By using freelancers as and when demand requires, organisations need only pay them for the hours they put in.

Writing with purpose

Left:
A typical creative studio interior. This one belongs to FEREF, the international marketing communications agency which produces a wide range of innovative publicity material for the entertainment business, promoting such items as new film releases and the latest computer games.

Now it's your turn

In addition to the famous international brands with their global advertising campaigns there are a host of other products and services that require promotion in order to raise awareness and stimulate desire among a wide variety of audiences.

Spend 30 minutes looking through a magazine, strolling through your local high street, or watching commercial television and make a list of the products, brands and services that you see being advertised and promoted.

Once you open your eyes and ears to all the promotional messages out there, you'll be amazed at the sheer scale and volume of advertising.

Word-check

Freelance copywriter – there's a romantic yet violent origin for this particular phrase which describes a writer who is hired on an occasional basis to help out at an agency or company.

The term 'freelance' originates from medieval mercenaries whose lances were available for hire to do battle on behalf of their paylord.

Just make sure you wield your mighty pen with care or you could have someone's eye out.

Where you find copywriters △ Copywriters as communicators

Right:
It might seem strange in a book on copywriting to show an advert that features a clever visual gag with few words beyond those on the label of the mayonnaise jar. However, this brilliant idea is a direct response to those very words on the jar: Hellmann's Extra Light and what they imply for anyone watching their weight.

Client: Hellmann's
Agency: Lowe London
Reproduced with kind permission of Unilever UK

Conveying ideas through words and pictures

In practice, coming up with ideas – or 'concepts', as they are grandly called in the advertising industry – is an important part of the copywriter's role. And with many concepts, the visual idea springs to mind at the same time as the headline. It's only natural that a concept should develop in this way since images tend to conjure up words in our heads while words paint pictures in our minds.

The traditional creative team within an ad agency consists of a copywriter and art director (which is a posh name for a designer – perhaps copywriters should be called text directors?). Whatever job titles they choose to use, the two members of this team need to develop a very close working relationship. It really doesn't matter who comes up with each idea just so long as, between you, some great ideas are generated.

And just as art directors and graphic designers don't have a monopoly on visual ideas, so copywriters aren't the only people who can come up with words. Headlines, straplines and captions are all up for grabs and if a designer produces some good copy, well, just make sure that you're receptive enough to appreciate it.

One of the greatest attributes that you need to encourage in yourself and others is the ability to recognise a good idea, wherever it might come from. It also helps if you are able to seize upon the creative potential within all ideas.

Very often a weak idea, or even a downright bad one, can be turned on its head or looked at from another angle and turned into a great idea. So, don't be too quick to jump to conclusions but remember to try and think laterally and explore all those other creative possibilities.

Word-check

Copywriting – a strange term for the original wording that copywriters are meant to produce since it suggests we're simply copying down words.

A quick trip to the dictionary and we discover that the word 'copy' derives from Middle English via old French with its roots in the Latin *copia* meaning a transcript or copy.

Moving on from medieval monks scratching away in their scriptoria, the word is now applied to any written material that fills the columns of a newspaper or provides the text for an advertisement.

If a picture is worth a thousand words why did I just have to tell you that using a sentence? And equally, isn't it possible for a word to suggest a thousand images?

Where you find copywriters ▷ Copywriters as communicators

If we want to be clever with words, it must always be with the aim of communicating the right message in a memorable way and with maximum impact.

Advertising copywriters are employed to convey messages and persuade people into a certain course of action, whether that is to feel tempted by a new aftershave, to realise the dangers of casual sex or to donate money to a children's charity.

It's therefore important for copywriters to be able to communicate their ideas successfully. And that quality of communication is not restricted to advertising copy alone; copywriters should also be able to write proposals and talk about their work clearly and persuasively. Once again, the ability to use language effectively is essential if you want to get your points across.

On a positive note for people wishing to climb the agency career ladder, this is one of the reasons why so many Creative Directors, Managing Directors and Chief Executives of advertising agencies turn out to have served their time as copywriters.

As a copywriter you are meant to have a good command of language and to have developed at least a basic understanding of marketing and consumer psychology. These practical skills not only enable you to come up with effective concepts but also to explain them concisely and precisely for the benefit of account handlers and clients alike.

Although advertising is a creative discipline, writers who work in this industry must never lose sight of the fact that we're putting words together for a particular purpose. Our intention is usually to increase awareness and sales of our clients' products, although our skills might equally be employed for other reasons. For example, some advertising is created to address public health concerns – perhaps to encourage people to give up a harmful habit such as smoking.

Whatever the purpose of the advertisement – and that requirement should be clearly stated in the 'brief' – we need to achieve effects that produce specific results. This means we have to shape our ideas and copy to suit that particular purpose.

Above:
Teddy gets ready for a night on the town. Actually this surreal image is intended to illustrate the bizarre and slightly disturbing combination of children's charities, safe sex and male scent – just to show you the variety of tasks copywriters might be asked to work on.

Word-check

Brief – a clear written instruction for the creative team, usually created by an agency's account management team working closely with the client's marketing personnel.

An advertising brief may take many forms but essentially it needs to describe *what*, *who*, *why*, and *where*. *What* it is you are going to be advertising, *who* you are advertising to, *why* you are carrying out this work, and *where* it's going to appear.

Oh, and there will also be some deadlines for the delivery of your material and a budget – just to stop you getting carried away with some over-elaborate and expensive advertising concepts such as painting the Eiffel Tower pink and transporting it to Brighton to promote *Gay Paree*.

Starting writing

Any copywriter who tells you that they're not a little bit frightened by a pen sitting on a blank sheet of paper, or an empty computer screen with its blinking cursor, is either lying or perhaps not too concerned about the quality of their work. OK, perhaps there are one or two exceptions; writers who can simply turn out perfect copy with the minimum of effort, but generally, copywriters worry about their abilities and are highly self-critical.

You've done it before but this is a new client and this particular ad campaign is aimed at a different audience. Will you be able to pull it off? Will your text meet the brief and succeed in being lively and persuasive? Will it appeal to the client? Even more importantly, will it appeal to their customers?

Apart from the reassuring fact that you're not alone in being concerned about your capabilities, maybe we all need that slight element of self-doubt to ensure we don't become complacent. It's our basic uncertainty and a desire to prove ourselves that makes us strive to create better work.

One encouraging tip I can give you is that it is possible to write yourself into a project. Make yourself a cup of coffee or tea, munch a biscuit or have a banana and then force yourself to start work. Even if you're feeling uninspired and your spirit's flagging, you can still begin to put thoughts down on paper and succeed in breaking through your writer's block.

Writing your way into a project can be a very effective way of uncluttering your mind and getting rid of vague ideas and weak expressions. For example, when asked to write body copy, it's surprising how often, after a brief moment of reflection, your second sentence becomes your first – and your first is scrapped.

However, we're really getting ahead of ourselves since, before we can even think about writing, we need to engage in some serious research and consider such essentials as what it is we're meant to be promoting and to whom. In other words, we need to learn more about the product's features and benefits and analyse exactly who it is we're talking to.

To find out more about these basic requirements you can turn to Chapter Two: Understanding your product and Chapter Three: Knowing your audience. In the meantime, I've got a few more tips and ideas for you on the following pages.

Left:
The lonely figure of the freelance
copywriter can be imagined
hunched over his keyboard
desperately struggling to fill a
blank page with brilliant ideas,
sustained only by a mug of tea,
a couple of biscuits and Radio 4.

**The very act of starting writing
can help clear your mind of some
of your more obvious thoughts.
Your subsequent ideas will often
flow more freely and demonstrate
greater originality.**

While advertising is usually about promoting a specific product or service, we're often dealing in ideas and emotions that are intended to create a more complex response in our audience.

There's an old saying in the advertising industry that talks about 'selling the sizzle not the steak' which seems a bit strange until you break down the meaning of this phrase.

Yes, of course we're trying to sell the steak but what is often most effective in promoting this or any other product is our ability to conjure up a mood or a desire that is linked to smell and taste and sound and sensation – and which makes this steak particularly memorable and desirable to our audience.

This marketing idea was first stated in such a sensational way in 1936 when Elmer Wheeler, a successful American salesman and motivational speaker (well, North America is the spiritual home of the hard-sell) wrote: 'It is the sizzle that sells the steak and not the cow, although the cow is, of course, mighty important'.

Putting more excitement into your advertising by 'selling the sizzle' might seem a rather artificial process but it's not simply a question of surrounding your product with meaningless razzamatazz. Ideally you need to bring out an attractive and appealing aspect which already exists within the product and emphasise the positive and emotional benefits of that particular feature.

Our emotions and desires are powerful forces that play a large part in how we behave as consumers of products and services.

Writing with purpose

Left:
This long-lasting campaign for Bisto gravy granules has emphasised the pleasure of the product's savoury taste and smell. The air-sniffing Bisto Kids saying 'Aah! Bisto' were originally created by the cartoonist Will Owen way back in 1919. This recent ad concentrates on a return to traditional family values, encouraging parents to commit to sitting down with their family for a hot meal with 'real Bisto gravy' – all shown in what appears to be a legally-binding document.

Client: Bisto
Agency: McCann-Erickson

Left:
There are many different ways to sell the sizzle. Recent TV ads by McCann-Erickson for Wall's Sausages feature a terrier that attacks his owners to get at the sausages. This remarkable dog can also say 'Wall's' rather than 'sausages' – which older readers might well remember from the BBC TV's *That's Life* programme.

Client: Wall's
Agency: McCann-Erickson

Copywriters as communicators △ Creating an emotional response

Right:
Self-indulgence or caring for
your fellow man? Advertising
is called upon to promote some
very different causes – from the
selfish to the selfless. Here a
clever cut-out direct-mail piece
highlights the insignificance
of many door-drop leaflets as
compared to the importance
of blood donation. The other
promotional leaflets that appear
below the National Blood
Service mailer are actually
a physical part of this item.

Client: National Blood Service
Agency: Kitcatt Nohr
Alexander Shaw
Copywriter: Simon Robinson
Art Director: Maya Rowson

Time for a reality check

At the risk of sounding all literary and
pretentious, I'm now going to quote a poet.
In his *Four Quartets*, TS Eliot writes:
'Human kind cannot bear very much
reality'. I think this simple statement
is a very revealing way to consider how
individuals react to life in general, and how
they respond to advertising in particular.

The fact that so much of everyday life
can seem a bit bland and lacking in
significance – especially to people living
relatively comfortable lives in affluent
countries – means that consumers show
a willingness and even a desire to meet
advertisers at least halfway in their
depiction of a more glamorous and
emotionally-charged world.

For example, waking up in the morning,
wiping the sleep from your eyes and
scratching your arse, it's likely to be a
far more pleasurable experience if you
get into the shower with a 'body wash'
that supposedly has the magical power to
turn you into a bright, alert individual who
is irresistible to the opposite sex, rather
than simply using a basic soap product
that gets rid of some of the grime.

The fantasy is much more attractive and far
more enriching than the mundane reality.
Well, we can all dream – and we frequently
do daydream about being more attractive,
intelligent and desirable. Much of
advertising aims to feed these fantasies –
or prey on our insecurities – and we're
happy to bask in the glow of such positive
self-images even if we are deluding
ourselves in the process.

On a more positive and less self-indulgent
note, it's also possible for advertising
to encourage us to be better people
and behave in a more generous way.
For example, some adverts suggest that
we could gain a warm feeling by giving
money to a worthy charity or donating
blood to the National Blood Service.
Thankfully, it's not all about greed, vanity
and the acquisition of material goods.

Writing with purpose

Right:
In the same way that Clark Kent can enter a phone box and emerge as a superhero, so advertising persuades us that a yawning wreck can leave the shower cubicle transformed into a sex god.

Showering you with compliments

As an example of emotive, aspirational writing, here's my version of the style that advertising copywriters adopt when we're asked to describe a shower-wash product aimed at young men. (Ideally, we need a moody black-and-white photo of David Beckham caressing his torso at this point.)

You know the kind of thing I mean. As you can see from the following text that I've knocked together – sorry, carefully crafted – it's much more than just describing the basic features of soap:

Renew your vitality with Sports Xtreme, the mineral-enriched shower gel with the natural power to transform your energy levels, leaving you invigorated, refreshed – and ready for total action.

One of my favourite examples of this type of over-the-top writing was a shower gel that claimed to have been 'developed with athletes' – as if the special and hitherto unknown scientific abilities of some unnamed sports stars had been used in the lab to create an effective soap product.

Or maybe they meant that bits of your favourite footballer, sprinter and pole vaulter were ground up and added to the shower gel for that extra element of sportiness!

Still, it's amazing how attractive and persuasive some of these statements can be. Once again we're selling the sizzle not the steak – and people are buying that sizzle by buying into the fantasy.

Why should the fact that a sports star has been involved in the development or promotion of a shower gel make it any more desirable or appealing? The truth is we're hoping at some conscious or unconscious level that some of the athleticism, sexiness and glamour of this individual will rub off on us – as we rub the soap products in.

A great deal of advertising seeks to tap into our aspirations and glamorise otherwise mundane areas of our lives. Suddenly a shower can seem a richly rewarding experience.

Writing with purpose

Word-check

Complement – don't confuse this word with 'compliment', which is when you want to praise someone or 'pay them a compliment' such as, 'That's a lovely hat; it really suits you officer' but not if you're trying to say something goes well with something else.

'Complement', on the other hand, is the word you need to use when one item enhances another. For example, 'That hat is pretty and it really complements your policeman's jacket'. In the same way, strong imagery can complement a great headline.

Meanwhile, the word 'complimentary' means free of charge, or provided with our compliments, such as a free ride in a police car.

Now it's your turn

How about an exercise to get you stretching your verbal creativity? Let's take some fairly standard products and make them sexy or at least more emotionally fulfilling than they might be without some inspirational words and images to give them a lift.

The choice is yours. You can work on a fizzy lemon-flavoured drink, a scented shaving foam, or a low-calorie chocolate bar. Better yet, why not create some packaging text for all three products?

And if it's not too much trouble, try coming up with some emotionally-charged and sensual product names for these items as well just to give them even more shelf appeal.

Copywriters as communicators △ Creating an emotional response

No matter what you're asked to advertise, it helps to keep an open and inquiring mind that's able to concentrate attention on the specific product and its benefits.

While your burning desire might be to work on the latest and most expensive TV and poster campaigns for Coca-Cola or Nike, the reality is that you're going to have to work on the accounts you're given. Depending on the ad agency or design consultancy employing your services, those accounts are not always going to seem particularly glamorous – or be ones you'd like to boast about to your mates down the pub.

What you might be asked to promote could vary from a packet of cereal to a toilet cleaner, or from a road safety campaign to an insurance company. However, you need to show the same level of enthusiasm for every brief that comes your way. And don't be too quick to dismiss whatever product or service it is that you've been asked to work on.

Sometimes it's easier to come up with some clever and interesting ideas for out-of-the-way or more unusual products. A strongly-branded product with a history of well-known advertising can prove restrictive and force you to work within some very constraining briefs. (Yes, there is an easy joke there concerning tight underwear but it's too obvious to exploit.)

Maybe I'm a bit odd but, whether it's a high-profile branded good or an obscure little item, I'm sufficiently interested in the weird byways of industry and commerce to relish finding out all about it. Whatever the item, the process of investigating that particular product – and what benefits it is supposed to deliver to its purchasers – is one that can prove fascinating.

Left:
This specialised business-to-business campaign on behalf of the Kiln reinsurance group – informing their international broker and risk management clients about their worldwide office expansion – benefits from an unexpected visual metaphor to demonstrate how this company is extending its reach.

Client: Kiln
Agency: College Design
Copywriter: Kate Rogers

Writing with purpose △ **Understanding your product** △ Knowing your audience

Understanding your product

Good ideas for your ad campaign will often grow from your product investigations. Remember, not all ad campaigns are built around solid products that you can see and touch. Some adverts will be for a service that you can't get hold of physically, for example, a life assurance policy, an annual gym membership, or a donation to a charity. Your task then is to try and make abstract benefits tangible and desirable.

And whether it's a product or a service, it's your job as the copywriter to learn as much as you can about the features and benefits of this particular item. Don't be shy about asking your account team or the client representatives some awkward – or even obvious – questions.

Too many people entering this profession are worried that they're going to look foolish if they ask silly questions. Well, some of your initial inquiries might seem naive to people with more experience in this product area than you, but, if it's something you don't know, you need to learn quickly. And generally, the only way to do that is to ask questions.

As the copywriter on the project, you're going to need all those answers before you can begin to consider creative ideas. After all, you're the poor sucker who, either on your own or in league with an art director, has to leave the meeting and come back with some concepts and copy lines that everyone else will then feel free to criticise.

Remember, the initial briefing meeting should not be the only opportunity you have to gain a better understanding of the product. Your account team should also be on hand to field further questions while, with luck, you'll be given the opportunity to quiz the client at greater length to clarify any details you're not sure about.

In some larger agencies where strategic planners are employed, you'll have another useful source of information. It's the role of such planners to research all aspects of the product, the market, potential customers, etc, and use that data to prepare a detailed brief and background information for the creative team to work on.

As someone new to a product, your innocence can be rewarding. After all, you might ask the obvious question that other people have overlooked.

Above:

Just because the product you're promoting is a database management program for a specialised audience doesn't mean your communication needs to be dull and technical. Despite some evidence to the contrary, database managers are human too and sometimes like to be entertained.

This mailshot for Microsoft's SQL Server featured a fold-over red acetate panel that magically revealed the obscured cartoon captions on the front cover:

Oh Brad, you're just too complex. I don't understand you.

Don't worry Marsha, there's an easy way to get your head around my data.

Client: Microsoft
SQL Server 2005
Agency: Mason Zimbler
Copywriter: Rob Bowdery

Creativity starts with research △ Applying your product knowledge

Taming the creative beast

Advertising creatives are sometimes kept shut away in the back room like wild animals who might upset the client with their uncouth habits and forthright questions. Any client liaison is then handled via the agency's supposedly more self-assured and diplomatic account management team. Occasionally, this can be an obstacle to obtaining a clear and detailed brief.

Unless the account handlers are particularly good at their job – and the best ones are very good – you can find yourself playing a game of 'Chinese whispers' where information isn't always relayed accurately. In the worst cases, you can end up working on a brief that has not been approved by the client, which means that your creative concepts are likely to be way off target.

As a copywriter, you sometimes have to make a bit of a nuisance of yourself – in the politest possible way of course. If there's stuff you don't understand or some more things you need to know, you just have to get hold of that information. If the account team can't provide it, and even the client's personnel aren't sure, then you need to push for answers.

For example, to understand a company's production methods, you might need to see their factory in operation. To discover why their current clients appreciate their product, it would be useful to speak to them at first-hand. Some creative directors and studio heads get annoyed at such attention to detail and this desire to learn more. They feel that a general overview should be enough for anybody.

These are the people who think that having a blank canvas and no preconceptions is the best approach to a brief. They only want to look at the 'big picture'. I suppose there is a danger of overloading your mind with too much information – but the skill lies in judging just what is relevant and what key facts might lead to some successful creative ideas.

With too much data to assimilate, you might not be able to 'see the wood for the trees' and yet sometimes you need to analyse those individual trees to see how the wood has developed and exactly how it functions. Personally, and if time allows, I like a lot of detail so I can pick out some strong-selling messages that might otherwise get overlooked.

Creative people work in subtly different ways. With luck and perseverance you'll get to work with like-minded creatives and encourage each other to generate some great ideas.

Above:
Even manufacturing processes and complex mechanical installations can provide an insight into how a product can deliver benefits to customers, particularly if you're promoting the idea of technical superiority to a highly sophisticated and knowledgeable audience.

Image courtesy of Spirax Sarco.

Word-check

Account handlers – each client company or specific product represented by an ad agency or design consultancy is called an 'account'. Within larger agencies, account handlers/managers/directors are the individuals employed to liaise between the client and the agency, where their role is to establish the brief, present creative work and generally make sure the client remains happy and informed.

Scruffy-looking creatives tend to adopt a studied nonchalance and cling to casual clothing. For a time you could tell the creative male of the species because they all wore an unofficial uniform of faded jeans and leather jackets while a popular current style is to have shaven heads and wear anything black.

Anyway, these sartorially-challenged creatives often call account handlers 'suits' on account of the smarter clothes they wear and the more formal approach they must adopt in front of clients. And that greater formality is useful since snorting in disgust in response to a client's comments – which some feisty creatives are apt to do – is generally frowned upon in meetings.

Creativity starts with research ▷ Applying your product knowledge

Be aware of everything that's gone before in terms of your client's advertising and that of their rivals and you can build your ideas on the back of that all-round knowledge.

Gaining all the right information

Research can take many forms but it's always a good idea to review any advertising that has previously been carried out for your client, whether by your agency or any other agencies that formerly worked on the account.

This will show you what's been done before and give you an informed starting point. Sometimes there's already a successful campaign up and running and you simply need to develop the next idea that builds upon the same theme.

I say 'simply,' but it isn't always easy coming up with ideas that match the excellence of a long-running campaign. *The Economist* series, created by Abbott Mead Vickers, is a case in point. Which is why I've kindly set it as a personal challenge for you in 'Now it's your turn'.

Alternatively, your client might be looking for an entirely fresh approach. Under such circumstances it's still essential to understand what's gone before to ensure that your ideas are radically, or at least sufficiently, different in your new campaign.

Don't restrict your investigations to your client and their advertising alone. It's extremely useful to review what your client's competitors have been up to in terms of advertising and promotional activities to see if you can learn some valuable lessons. That way you can avoid presenting your client with something one of their rivals has already done – *unless you can do it much better!*

I'll have more to say about originality later in this book so I'll just restrict myself to making the point that, when it comes to developing fresh ideas, it's not always necessary or indeed advisable to try and reinvent the wheel.

Sometimes you can pinch the wheels off an old idea, and maybe remodel them with a trendy set of alloys or some funky all-weather tyres, and you're ready to roll out your exciting 'new' campaign.

Understanding your product

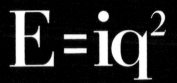

$$E = iq^2$$

The Economist

If more women read
The Economist, there'd be
fewer jobs for the boys.

The Economist

It's not what
you read at university
that counts.

The Economist

Read by
best-sellers.

The Economist

Left:
An established campaign which
achieves instant recognition
with its strong use of white text
reversed out of red to echo
the magazine's own masthead.
And look, the ads rely on witty
copy rather than fancy imagery
to make their point.

Creative Teams
from top to bottom:
Sean Doyle and Dave Dye,
David Abbott and Ron Brown,
Tim Riley and Peter Gausis,
Rob Bowdery

Now it's your turn

Witty, intelligent and thought-provoking:
the many ad treatments that have been
used in support of *The Economist*
campaign are a hard act to follow.

So now I'd like you to follow that act.
Just to prime the pump here are several
previous examples, plus I've also added in
one of my own. (Well, I don't want readers
to think I can't do the job.)

The brief is quite straightforward:
to persuade more readers through your
clever wordplays that a subscription to
The Economist is the sign of an intelligent
and successful business person.

Creativity starts with research △ Applying your product knowledge

Many adverts – presumably taking their lead from clients who are bursting with pride over their product's features or rejoicing in the construction of their new factory – simply bang on about obscure technical attributes or their amazing manufacturing prowess without conveying the practical benefits that those features and sophisticated processes are meant to offer to potential purchasers.

You're then left with an advert that's a dry account of technical features, and you've missed a major opportunity. After all, one practical way to inject more emotion into your advertising is to take a product's features and turn them into benefits. Having said that, I suppose I'd better try and show you what I mean.

An example of this might be a particularly efficient breaking system in a family car. Of course, you could talk about the vehicle's 'efficient disc brakes complete with automatic anti-lock braking system (ABS)' – or you could describe a dramatic situation where a child has run out into the street: 'Drive another car – and you won't stop until it's too late'.

This approach can be particularly effective when used in a TV advertisement but can also be adapted for poster and press advertising. It might seem a bit blunt, but it can give your audience an emotional jolt that makes the reader or viewer realise the importance of effective braking as a safety feature that saves lives.

There was a good example of this kind of advertising produced way back in the early 1980s by the agency Wight Collins Rutherford Scott (why do so many ad agencies sound like firms of solicitors?). Copywritten by Andrew Rutherford and art directed by Ron Collins, this press ad picked up on the fact that Goodyear Grand Prix S tyres had achieved a slightly shorter stopping distance in official road tests.

The modest claim in the headline was: 'Our tyres only stop you 32" shorter than the others'. However, this low-key headline was supported by a series of images of pedestrians: a mother pushing a child in a pram, young children, cyclists and even a pet dog. Each image demonstrated that these figures took up approximately 32 inches (or 81 cms if you're young or European and want the metric equivalent). In other words, the improved stopping distance could mean the difference between life and death.

As a section of the advert's body copy put it:

It's not an enormous amount in scientific terms. But translate that into human terms and it could easily mean the difference between stopping safely or running into very serious trouble.

Above:
So, what's the best way of demonstrating the stopping distance of your car? And why should we care? Well, it's up to the advertiser to make us care.

Checking your facts

In addition to run-outs of previous adverts, copies of product brochures – as well as any relevant rivals' promotional material – there's always the Internet where you can pursue your inquiries about a product or service that you've been asked to promote. This is an excellent source of information but you need to be as careful with this resource as with any other medium.

Not everything you find on the Internet is accurate. But then again, there's no guarantee of truth in any written material, whether in book or digital form. You have to rely in part on your own judgement, retain a cynical mind and then check any information against other sources to try and determine the truth.

Taking a product feature and turning it into a customer benefit is one of the copywriter's most useful techniques but it must be done well to make the idea convincing and compelling.

Creativity starts with research △ Applying your product knowledge △ Picking up on the details

If your client has managed to develop an original concept that delivers a practical benefit then you can build an entire campaign around that unique feature.

Sucked in by powerful advertising

Unique Selling Points or Unique Selling Propositions – it all depends on how you expand the acronym USPs – are often sought by account handlers and creative teams so we can claim a marketing distinction for this particular product and exploit a unique sales advantage over rivals' products. It's obviously a powerful and persuasive tool if you can demonstrate such a distinctive benefit and it's likely to form the primary message in your advertising campaign. The task of the creative team is then to turn that unique product advantage into a clear benefit statement.

An example of a unique selling point was the introduction of the bag-less cleaner by Dyson using that company's new cyclone technology. This innovative system supposedly meant 'no loss of suction' during prolonged use and that advantage has been promoted heavily in this company's advertising as a unique proposition. This new process also does away with an internal bag to collect the dust which accumulates instead in a clear plastic cylinder.

The fact that to maintain good suction, you need to clean dust out of the machine's filters every so often – and even frequently if you're picking up fine dust – doesn't appear to affect this company's claims that their machines 'do not lose suction'.

The Advertising Standards Authority certainly defends the right of Dyson to promote their product using the USP 'no loss of suction'. Whatever the power of this claim, a major additional marketing benefit appears to have been the funky design of this cleaner and the fact that you could see the dirt as you sucked it up.

It's just a shame that the process of getting rid of the dirt and dust you've collected involves the messy business of tipping it out of the nice clear bin into a nasty plastic bag. Which rather defeats the purpose of the cleaner being bag-less in the first place!

Understanding your product

2 TREE FERNS £470
SLATE
WATER FEATURE £60
LARGE HAMMOCK £48

GREEN NEIGHBOURS:
PRICELESS

MasterCard

There are some things money can't buy.
For everything else there's MasterCard.

Above:
This long-running campaign for MasterCard demonstrates the many items you can buy with this credit card while also enjoying the 'priceless' feelings that are the spin-off result. A fine example of promoting the emotional benefits of a product or service.

In this treatment, the ad suggests that the 'priceless' benefit of buying products for your garden will be the green envy generated among your neighbours.

Client: MasterCard
Agency: McCann-Erickson

Creativity starts with research ▷ Applying your product knowledge ▷ Picking up on the details

When is a USP not a USP?

Not all selling points that advertisers choose to promote are unique, but instead simply offer a strong proposition that a campaign can be built around. For example, it might be that a make of car wants to emphasise the safety aspect of their vehicles.

It doesn't necessarily matter if other cars have equally effective ABS braking systems, crumple zones, multiple airbags, etc, just so long as, through the power of the adverts, the consumer is readily able to associate a particular brand name with a feeling of safety and security – which also sneakily tends to suggest that all other makes of car might be less safe.

Yes, it's great if some independent scientific test singles out your client's vehicle for praise as having the best safety features in its class. That recognition alone can be the basis for an entire campaign, but it's not essential to have such external corroboration.

Mere suggestion can work its magic in advertising. We're not allowed to make wildly inaccurate claims – the Advertising Standards Authority would slap our wrists and pull our ads. However, we are clever at being persuasive and making the most of a minor benefit or a small advantage to set our product above and apart from the competition in the minds of our audience.

USPs can prove extremely useful in formulating concepts and setting a product apart from its competitors – which is a major advantage for advertising agencies desperately looking for an original angle.

Above and left:
While not necessarily unique – in that there are other 'natural' products with no artificial additives – Yoplait fromage frais benefits here from a very clever and clear demonstration of the purity of their offering: Petits Filous (the name means Little Rascals) is produced for young children to eat – while the ads are aimed at their naturally concerned parents.

Client: Yoplait
Agency: McCann-Erickson

Word-check

Unique – be careful when you use this word. Unique is an absolute expression. Either something is unique – the only one of its kind – or it's not. Something rare could be 'almost unique' but it's not possible or indeed necessary for anything to be 'very unique'.

As we've seen from the explanation of Unique Selling Propositions (USPs), while it's useful if a product benefit is indeed unique, we can still work up an attractive selling proposition from a feature that happens to be shared among several competitors.

Of course some things are even rarer than unique, such as hen's teeth, rocking-horse poo or an amusing quip from Chris Moyles.

Creativity starts with research △ Applying your product knowledge △ Picking up on the details

There are many modern examples of advertising in this book, but I would like to pay my respects to some old masters, since there are many lessons to be learnt when we recall what has been done before.

On the subject of exploring a product in detail, picking up on a relatively minor feature and then exploiting that feature with great style, there have been few better examples than David Abbott's death-defying lying-down-in-the-face-of-a-Volvo ad.

The Volvo car was shown suspended in the air at an alarming angle over the prone figure of a man. This image on its own was intriguing enough while the headline also drew you in: 'If the welding isn't strong enough, the car will fall on the writer.'

Not a particularly sexy feature you might think, but apparently the individual welds on this Volvo 740 were strong enough to support the weight of the entire car. What was probably a throwaway comment by one of the technicians led to an idea of how to demonstrate the overall strength of the car.

There's an element of circus showmanship by having the writer take up position below the dangling car. It's like the head in the lion's mouth, the figure about to be fired from a cannon, the pretty girl in a spangly swimsuit hanging only by her teeth – and because of that element of entertainment and suspense the ad succeeds in making its point in a truly memorable way.

Furthermore, by physically involving himself in the advert, the writer is providing his personal endorsement. It makes the entire ad more believable and he can justifiably write at first-hand of his experiences in support of the Volvo's manufacturing strength. The body copy reads:

That's me, lying rather nervously under the new Volvo 740.

For years I've been writing in advertisements that each spot weld in a Volvo is strong enough to support the weight of the entire car.

Someone decided I should put my body where my mouth is. So we suspended the car and I crawled underneath.

Of course the Volvo lived up to its reputation and I lived to tell the tale.

But the real point of the story is this; the Volvo 740 may have a different body shape, a fast and frugal new engine, a new interior and a new suspension system, but in one respect it's just like the Volvos of yore.

It's so well built you can bet your life on it.

I know. I just did.'

It's a bit of a stretch trying to cram in all those new features of the Volvo: body shape, engine, interior and suspension. I also think the olde-worlde 'Volvos of yore' phrase should have been strangled at birth, my liege – but the key idea you come away with is expressed precisely and accurately in the line: 'It's so well built you can bet your life on it'.

MUM-TO-BE ON BOARD

VOLVO

for life

NOT EVERY PASSENGER WEARS A SEATBELT

VOLVO
for life

TO VOLVO, THEY'RE ALREADY A PASSENGER

An eye for detail and a nose for a good marketing story can pick out powerful messages from the smallest features.

Above:

Here's a modern take on Volvo advertising: a direct-mail pack which achieves great impact on the subject of impact protection. This striking campaign grew out of the fact that Volvo tests its cars using a 'pregnant' crash-test dummy.

The Creative Director's wife was pregnant at the time of this brief so there was a degree of personal interest which translated perfectly into this creative solution, which highlights the fact that Volvo takes care of its passengers – even before they're born. There's even a handy 'Mum-to-be on board' window sticker – with the more usual 'Baby on board' wording on the reverse.

Agency: EHS Brann
Creative Director:
Frazer Howard

Applying your product knowledge ▷ Picking up on the details

Another old master

I suppose we can't talk about adverts based on product details without giving a mention to David Ogilvy and that oft-raised – and equally often-praised – Rolls-Royce ad from 1958 that was headlined: 'At 60 miles an hour the loudest noise in this new Rolls-Royce comes from the electric clock.'

(Sorry but we seem to be stuck on cars at the moment. I'll try and avoid any further references to motor vehicles in the rest of this book.) Once again it's a case of looking at the fine detail, picking up on a reviewer's report and using one salient point to represent an entire manufacturing ethos.

Perhaps the dashboard clock had a very loud tick, but most people will take away the sense that this car is so well-built, so carefully engineered – with its snug-fitting doors and windows, its highly efficient and well-tuned engine, its smooth suspension, etc – that, even when travelling at a fair old lick, the new Rolls-Royce simply purrs along.

It's that attention to just one detail which manages to suggest all those other attributes of superb engineering. It's also as if the advertising copywriter himself has taken the same level of care and consideration in analysing the benefits of this vehicle. The headline is beautifully understated and yet manages to convey the comfort and opulence of this prestigious car.

That understatement is also a subtle reflection of the car's well-bred British branding. It appears to be saying 'our engineers have created the height of excellence but we don't need to shout about it. Instead we go about our business quietly – just as the car travels swiftly yet softly and reliably'.

As an aside, it's worth pointing out that, according to his own opening paragraph in this advert, David Ogilvy came across this nugget of information from a review published by the editor of a motor magazine:

'At 60 miles per hour, the loudest noise comes from the electric clock,' reports the Technical Editor of The Motor, the leading automotive publication in the United Kingdom.

The copywriting skill of David Ogilvy lay in his ability to recognise the value of that detail which he then turned into a highly effective headline.

Understanding your product

Left:
How might a copywriter persuade commuters to get out of their cars and onto their bikes?

Now it's your turn

You've seen how some past masters of copywriting have promoted motor vehicles. How about we go green and produce some effective advertising for the humble bicycle? Let's try and get people out of their cars and into the cycle lanes.

This is your chance to wheel out some words and recycle some images for a form of transport that doesn't harm the environment and keeps you fit while saving you lots of money.

Come on what are you waiting for? On your bike – and get writing!

Left:
The Rolls-Royce of advertising or how to seize the opportunity to turn a simple observation into a key selling point. Just recently a degree of doubt has been cast on the originality of David Ogilvy's Rolls-Royce headline. A 1930s press ad for Pierce-Arrow automobiles has been unearthed which states 'The only sound one can hear in the new Pierce-Arrow is the ticking of the electric clock'. Pure coincidence or an adman's old trick of recycling ideas?

Clever copywriters must remain open to chance encounters and be ready to pounce on unconsidered trifles. All you need is an inquiring mind – and a very large measure of lateral thinking.

Applying your product knowledge △ Picking up on the details

The place you felt safest no longer exists

You must understand who your potential customers are and then talk to them in a direct and personal way that engages their interest and makes them feel positive towards your product.

We're not very far into this book on copywriting and yet I think it's not too soon to trot out a standard truth about advertising. This point is so obvious it's a cliché – and this earth-shattering insight is that the reader, listener or viewer of your advert often has only one thought in mind, and that rather selfish consideration is 'What's in it for me?' or, to put it more politely, 'Why should I be interested in this?'

No one is going to be interested in your product or your advert unless they feel it addresses them directly, is relevant to their needs, entertains them – and ideally offers them a significant benefit that will improve their lives in some large or small way. Maybe it will save them money, give them more confidence, make them happier, feel more comfortable, more attractive, more intelligent.

Every now and then, as you're working on your advertising concepts, it's good to take time out to distance yourself from the agency and client account viewpoint and put yourself firmly into the shoes of your reader or viewer. Try and think like one of those potential customers and with fresh and slightly cynical eyes consider your concepts while chanting the mantra 'What's in it for me?'

Generally, people do not ask to view your advert. It tends to be a distraction or an interruption to whatever else they happen to be doing. A billboard by the side of the road, a TV commercial disrupting a favourite TV soap, an irritating pop-up on a website, a full-page ad in the middle of an interesting magazine article.

Unless you can convince them that your message is both entertaining and relevant, they're going to drive right past, go off and make a cup of tea, click their mouse, or simply turn the page.

Left:
This agency knows their customers very well. To promote the latest manifestation of Resident Evil, a loving and caring mother is replaced by a sinister image of an evil-looking ghoul. Perfectly shocking material for an audience of young boys who love the horror genre. 'Now go and tidy your room!'

Client: CAPCOM
Agency: OWN+P
Creative Director:
James Sinclair
Copywriter: Neil Cook
Art Director: Jason Fairclough

Understanding your product ▷ **Knowing your audience** ▷ Mastering the language

As soon as you start working in advertising – or indeed any branch of marketing – you're going to hear the term 'target audience' a great deal. It has to be one of the two major preoccupations for anyone trying to develop creative concepts and write effective copy.

The first big consideration is **what** you're advertising – the product or service – which we've looked at in the previous chapter, and the second is **to whom**. All advertising and marketing can be reduced to that key and apparently simple question: 'What are we promoting to whom?' (Of course it's not so easy coming up with effective advertising answers to that question!)

Despite the simplicity of this aspect of advertising, there are some hideously complicated text books dealing with marketing and media theory whose authors seem intent on bamboozling their readers while making their subjects as obscure and complicated as possible.

Such texts are packed with dense marketing jargon, peppered with psycho-linguistic babble and spiced with pseudo-scientific equations where A = Market Share, B = Propensity to Purchase, Y = Consumer Spending Power and Z = the Reader's Eyes Closing. It's all a bit strange when we're meant to be in the business of clear communication.

However, one of the hardest tasks for any writer is to explain things simply and pare ideas down to their bare essentials. Which is what I'm trying to do here with my summary of advertising: 'What to whom?' – that is the question.

OK there are some other niceties, such as the particular message you wish to convey and where your advertising is going to appear, but in essence, understanding the product and its intended audience is at the heart of all our endeavours.

You must never lose sight of your audience. Your task is to develop a familiarity with their hopes, concerns, wishes and desires. Then you need to develop the kind of ideas and adopt the style of language that they will understand and respond to positively.

It's not always easy to get under the skin of a senior accountant one day and into the mind of a teenager the next. However, as an advertising copywriter, you've got to try and adopt a suitable persona and speak to these people – whoever they might be – directly and persuasively.

Knowing your audience

deliver us from evil

The Salvation Army wants to be there for every life destroyed by drug abuse.
But we need your help. salvationarmy.org.uk

Annual Appeal

GOODNESS
LOVE FAMILY HOPE TRUST
SACRIFICE
FAITH CARE FRIENDSHIP
COMMITMENT

Left:
Despite the fact that the 'Sally Army' is a well-known charitable institution, there was a fear that in an increasingly secular society a strongly Christian creative approach, while appealing to some of their target audience, might alienate other potential donors.

Research indicated that many people appreciated traditional Christian values – such as commitment, care, sacrifice and family – and yet would prefer these ideas presented in a more subtle way. Overall there was a need for a more modern view of The Salvation Army's work.

This new creative approach was launched with a poster campaign that used individual phrases taken from what must be the most familiar Christian prose in the English language: The Lord's Prayer. The posters featured gritty and realistic portrayals of drug addiction, child cruelty, elderly abuse and homelessness, demonstrating the immediacy and relevance of The Salvation Army's work.

Client: The Salvation Army
Campaign: Deliver us from evil
Agency: Target Direct

Left:
Do you understand the customers you're trying to influence and could you pick them out in a crowd? More importantly, could they pick your ad out in a similarly crowded marketplace?

Who are the individuals that make up your target audience, what is their level of understanding, and what do you want them to take away from your advertisement?

Staying on target △ Can you rely on market research?

Are you talking to me?

While market research companies have been active in advertising for many years, it is only relatively recently that new techniques have made their categorisation and commentaries more realistic than the simplistic 'Social Grade A = Upper middle class higher managerial types', etc. The addition of lifestyle and behavioural characteristics has proved especially useful for direct marketing companies who wish to compile and maintain accurate mailing lists of likely consumers.

The truth is that crude class and employment categories do not necessarily provide a good indication of an individual's actual interests and spending habits. For example, although a leisure pursuit such as scuba diving, skiing or paragliding might once have been considered a fairly elitist and affluent activity, it pays advertisers to recognise that many different types of people are now liable to engage in such hobbies.

So, there's no reason why a male sheep-farmer from Yorkshire and a female doctor from Devon shouldn't share a fondness for scuba diving despite the fact that they come from very different backgrounds, have had very different educations and doubtless draw down very different wages.

But how do you target these disparate people who happen to have one common interest? Ideally, rather than using some basic demographics (age, sex, income, location, etc) to try and predict the types of people who are most likely to develop a penchant for swimming with the fishes, you need to spot when they're doing it, or planning to do it.

In other words, you need to pick up on who's buying scuba gear, who's subscribing to diving publications and who's travelling off to the Red Sea for a spot of underwater activity. Of course, you can always advertise to a number of these people via specialist diving and adventure holiday magazines. Alternatively, you can seek to obtain their personal details: name, address, e-mail address etc, and start sending them relevant information directly to their homes. Direct marketing can be very personal – and highly effective.

If all your advertising communications are targeted to the right recipients then there's no reason for anyone to complain of 'junk mail'. In fact they'll probably be pleased to receive your relevant marketing material.

Word-check

Direct marketing – direct marketing covers a great deal more than mailshots – sometimes derided or dismissed as 'junk mail' – which can now be very cleverly targeted and personalised to the individual recipient.

In fact, direct marketing includes a wide range of advertising activities, from mailshots to e-shots and encompasses any form of promotional activity that includes a direct response mechanism, which encourages individuals to interact and become more involved with your message.

The direct response mechanism can be a coupon at the bottom of a press ad, or a telephone number and website address either printed at the foot of a poster, or announced in a TV commercial or radio ad. Modern digital technology permits an even greater degree of interactivity where viewers can respond immediately to register their interest – or even buy – online.

Below and right:
Can you tell exactly which kind of person is going to be interested in spending a great deal of money and much of their spare time dressing up in rubber?

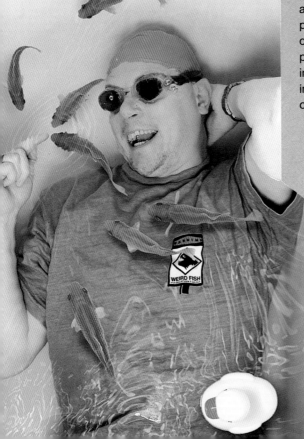

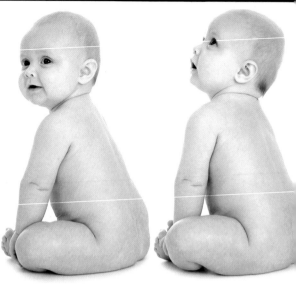

How well do you need to know your audience?

Some writers find it helpful to think of one representative member of a particular audience and then address their concepts and copy to that individual.

Although this holds true for some forms of direct marketing, for example, the closely targeted mailpack where we have a great deal of personal information about the recipient, you can become carried away with the notion of individual communication when it comes to other forms of advertising media.

A poster campaign doesn't have to talk directly to one individual to work well. A big, bold and cheeky statement such as the Wonderbra's 'Hello Boys' had wide appeal because it seemed to empower women to assert and flaunt their sexuality while also pandering to a male preoccupation with ladies' chests.

In this example, I don't think the writer sat down with a complex demographic breakdown of his audience and then focussed all his attention on one woman he happened to know, who he thought matched the planner's profile most closely.

So, the good news for copywriters is that we don't have to get bogged down in the finer details of who makes up our audience. For instance, it's usually enough to know that we're talking to parents who require nappies for their babies or car drivers who might benefit from an improved screenwash, or whatever.

In such cases, it might help to understand that the typical parent who buys nappies is female, between the ages of 18 and 35 and is mainly concerned about her child's comfort and her own household expenditure, while in terms of car drivers who'd like to have a smear-free windscreen, well, that's likely to be anyone who drives a car. Fairly obvious innit?

Now you just need to come up with some very clever creative concepts and copylines which will sell a shed-load of nappies and screenwash. Which is when it begins to get tough.

A great deal of marketing and advertising is simply applied common sense. But then again, maybe common sense isn't such a common commodity.

Knowing your audience

Left:
Market research has its place but a baby's bottom needs a nappy and it's not hard to know what's going through a parent's mind when it comes to buying such products: price, comfort, absorbency, and maybe a bit of environmental concern.

Word-check

Above-the-line and **below-the-line** – these old-fashioned terms are still used to describe two supposedly different forms of advertising: 'above-the-line' represents high-profile ads, such as TV, radio, posters and print, while 'below-the-line' indicates material such as sales literature and direct mail: items previously held in low regard by larger agencies.

Ad agencies originally gained a large financial commission when placing ads in the press or on TV which meant creative work did not need to be charged out to the client. The story goes that these terms developed from some form of accounting system where TV and press advertising fell 'above-the-line' whereas creative work on brochures etc was chargeable and appeared 'below-the-line'.

Nowadays the term 'above-the-line' tends to be used loosely to describe any mass media advertising. Meanwhile many companies try to develop integrated advertising campaigns that work 'through-the-line' across a wide variety of media forms.

Now it's your turn

Having established the truth about nappies and screenwash it would seem churlish not to ask you to come up with your creative ideas for campaigns in support of these two products.

So, set down your thoughts for some concepts and headlines that will have maximum audience appeal. In terms of media placement, I'll ask that you concentrate on posters and full-page magazine ads.

Since I haven't named the brands, I'll also ask you to come up with suitable product names for these items. And just in case you felt tempted, you're not allowed to call them Nappo or Screeno.

Staying on target △ Can you rely on market research?

A serious flaw with some forms of market research – such as research groups, consumer panels, etc – is that you don't always get accurate and honest answers from the people involved. People have an annoying habit of saying one thing and then doing another. It's not necessarily an intentional deception but more of a self-deception.

Remember what I said about our tendency to lead fantasy lives in our heads? (If not, please pay attention.) Anyway, just to recap, we're inclined to be fantasists who like to think well of ourselves – and who want other people to think well of us too. (Or maybe you're a sociopath or psychopath, in which case we can rule you out of our discussions anyway, unless we're trying to market chainsaws and bin liners.)

In truth, we might be so stingy or suspicious that we never give any money away to a good cause but if we're asked a question about our charitable giving, we're apt to say 'Oh yes, I do my bit'. Then again, ask a larger person if he or she eats a lot of cake and it's often a case of, 'Oh no, I prefer salads'. Who are we kidding – and yet we want to be seen to be thinking and doing the right thing.

Furthermore, testing ad campaigns by showing them to a customer panel is fraught with problems because people are often fearful or puzzled by anything new or different.

Your hard-hitting, edgy campaign can end up being reined back due to a lack of imagination on the part of your particular panel of consumers.

Another weakness is that a strong personality can sometimes exert too great an influence over other members of a panel. The independence of those individuals is then compromised as they end up meekly going along with the dominant voice.

Despite my reservations that research panels have a tendency to be a brake on creativity and originality, and aren't always to be trusted, they aren't all bad. A research panel might just highlight a serious flaw in your thinking.

However, the most reliable research that you can base future marketing and advertising activity upon is actual consumer behaviour. In other words, it's not what your customers say, but what they do. And even then, people's buying habits can change over time, or a new product can suddenly and surprisingly become very popular, putting previously established brands in the shade.

Your customer is a fickle and frustrating animal, who will often tell you what you want to hear – and then go away and do something entirely different.

Knowing your audience

Tesco Stores Ltd
Registered Office
Tesco House, Delamare Road
Cheshunt, Herts. EN8 9SL
www.tesco.com

VAT NO: 220430231

THANK YOU FOR SHOPPING
WITH US

TESCO
CLUBCARD

We've missed you recently;
so we're offering you a little thank you
to welcome you back in-store.
We look forward to seeing you soon.
If you have any questions
please call 0800 59 16 88.
Please remember to use your coupon
before the end date.

Tesco Stores Ltd
Registered Office
Tesco House, Delamare Road
Cheshunt, Herts. EN8 9SL
www.tesco.com

VAT NO: 220430231

THANK YOU FOR SHOPPING
WITH US

TESCO
CLUBCARD

We've missed you recently;
so we're offering you a little thank you
to welcome you back in-store.

This coupon can only be exchanged for qualifying
purchases of goods or services equivalent to its face value,
or it can be exchanged for goods or services of a higher
value on payment of the difference, at any participating
Tesco store in the UK or IOM.

Purchases of tobacco products, Esso fuel, café, lottery
products, e-top up, prescription medicines, infant formulae
milk and gift vouchers are excluded.

Age restrictions may apply.

Customers must be 18 years or over to purchase alcohol.

Not redeemable through Tesco.com or Clubcard Great Deals.
From time to time other goods or services may be excluded,
if so notification will be given at point of sale.

This coupon has no cash value. No change given.

Copied, damaged or defaced coupons will not be accepted.

Valid until 07/08/05.

This voucher is and shall remain the property of
Tesco Stores Limited and is not for re-sale or publication.

TESCO

DEAR MRS SAMPLE
WHERE HAVE YOU BEEN?
IT'S NOT BEEN THE SAME WITHOUT
YOU AROUND

IF YOU COME BACK SOON I'LL GIVE
YOU £5 OFF YOUR SHOPPING WHEN
YOU SPEND £20 – AND IF I'M BUSY,
ONE OF MY FRIENDS WILL DO IT

HOPE TO SEE YOU IN THE NEXT
FEW DAYS

FROM TILL NUMBER 4

07/06/05 12:39 1234 567 8910 0000

★ ★ ★ ★ ★ ★ ★ ★ ★ ★ ★ ★ ★ ★

A LITTLE EXTRA FROM
CLUBCARD

£5 OFF

WHEN YOU SPEND £20 OR MORE
IN A SINGLE TRANSACTION

A Sample
123456 1234 1234 1234

Valid until 07/08/05

Please see over for
terms and conditions

9 914430 975009

★ ★ ★ ★ ★ ★ ★ ★ ★ ★ ★ ★ ★ ★

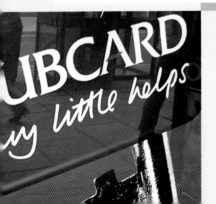

Above and left:
Tesco wanted to persuade
previously loyal customers
to return to their local
supermarkets. So they sent
lapsed customers a personal
message in the form of a
till receipt, telling them that
Tesco missed them – while
also providing a money-off
coupon to tempt them back.

A nice touch was to have this
customised till receipt written
as though check-out 4 was
personally missing you and
hoped to see you soon!

Client: Tesco Stores –
'Win back campaign'
Agency: EHS Brann
Creative Director: Nigel Clifton
Production Manager:
Peter Clarke
Database Agency: Dunnhumby

Staying on target △ Can you rely on market research? △ Adopting the right tone of voice

When market research goes wrong

We've investigated our product and we think we know what our audience likes so we're ready to make some terrific marketing decisions and develop some fantastic advertising campaigns. Right? Well, it doesn't always work out that way.

Back in the early 1980s the marketing people at Coca-Cola were a bit miffed when a greater proportion of people taking the 'Pepsi Challenge' in a blind taste-test said they preferred the marginally sweeter flavour of Pepsi over Coke. At this time Coca-Cola was also losing market share to its rival.

Their response was to create a modified and sweeter version of their own product which they duly went out and tested on consumers. The response to this research was largely favourable with more people showing a preference for the new-style Coke.

The stage was set for the launch of new-recipe Coke. However, what the researchers had neglected to tell their consumers was that they were not only planning to introduce this new product but it was going to replace the old. In other words, traditional Coke was dead, long live new Coke.

The researchers and marketing people had reckoned without the extraordinary emotional attachment American consumers had with this product and what it represented in their lives – and the lives of their families. After all, this was Coca-Cola, the fizzy symbol of America, the drink whose festive seasonal adverts were alleged to have changed Santa Claus's costume from traditional green to Coca-Cola corporate red!

There was uproar, outrage and a demand for the old Coke to be reinstated no matter what the researchers' taste tests had revealed about their audience's preferred flavours. In the end, something positive for the Coca-Cola corporation came out of this marketing disaster. Old-style original recipe (well, not quite original since in its first guise there really were cocaine derivatives in the mix) Coke was given a major boost as it went back on sale.

It just goes to show that you don't only need to know what people like, but also what motivates them emotionally. Very often, we're not rational beings and our psychological make-up plays a large part in our purchasing behaviour.

This case study also demonstrates that spending a large sum of money on market research is no guarantee of success. You've got to ask the right questions and then interpret the answers with extreme caution.

Knowing your audience

Above:
Coca-Cola has created an extraordinary position for itself in the minds of its long-term consumers. The emotional attachment felt for this drink often goes well beyond its taste, tapping into a deep well of personal associations, shared memories and projected feelings.

Client: Coca-Cola

Caution: mess with a popular product at your peril and don't rely on market research unless you know you're asking all the right questions.

Having established who your audience are, and what is most likely to appeal to them, you now need to decide how you're going to talk to them.

When it comes to writing adverts, the best copywriters are chameleon-like in their ability to adopt a different persona, but how different is that from how we all tend to act in front of different audiences?

Would you use the same tone of voice and choice of language when talking to these various people: your close friends, your partner, your parents, your boss, your bank manager, the policeman who's stopped you for speeding, the magistrate who's about to hand down your sentence?

Your tone of voice and use of language depends on your audience and that can vary considerably in terms of the type and level of language they understand, as well as the impression you're trying to make.

It's sometimes helpful to think about the tone of voice used by different newspapers whose journalists adjust their style to appeal to their different readerships. Try and think of the tone and style adopted by *The Sun* versus *The Times*, or *The Daily Mail* versus *The Guardian*, etc.

Then consider how journalists would write up the same story for those different newspapers. Here's a sample of what I mean, where I've taken a typical summer heatwave story but written it up in two very different styles. Can you tell the subtle difference?

Hottest July since records began
The meteorological office reports that July has been the hottest on record with a mean temperature of 24 degrees Celsius (75 degrees Fahrenheit). There have been government warnings of hosepipe bans coming into force at the end of August unless significant rain falls in the next two weeks.

Stunning Suzy sizzles in the sun
Phwoar – it's enough to get anyone hot under the collar. Temperatures soared this month and it's no wonder as sultry Suzy and her sexy chums got down to the bare essentials and frolicked in the sea at Southend. If this is global warming, well, we say bring it on – and let's get 'em off.

Obviously, my first journalistic treatment was modelled on *The Times* while the second was cleverly modified for *The Church Times*.

Right:
There are many newspapers out there and they're targeted at different audiences. It can help you create the right tone of voice for your advertising by thinking about such journalistic styles.

Now it's your turn

Try taking a story from a 'serious' newspaper and rewriting it in the style of a more popular 'red-top' daily. It should be possible to have some fun with this exercise.

How can you make the story more immediate, punchier, snappier? What kind of headline will you use? How do you get the main points of the story across without losing dramatic impact?

Will you choose to emphasise just one aspect of the story? Will you try and seek out the comic possibilities in an otherwise serious report to appeal to a new audience?

Research can help you find out who it is you're meant to be talking to but it's up to you to adjust your tone of voice to try and appeal to that particular audience.

Can you rely on market research? △ Adopting the right tone of voice

Right:
Two tasks for Bovis Homes
where we had to try and appeal
to two very different audiences,
adjusting the tone of voice to
create a suitably persuasive
personality.

Client: Bovis Homes
Copywriter: Rob Bowdery
Designer: Charlotte Kidner

Adjusting your style of writing

Here are two samples of writing where I've adopted completely different tones of voice for two very different audiences. What these audiences have in common is that they're looking for a new home – or, at least, we hope we can persuade them to start looking in our direction.

The first writing sample is a direct marketing letter aimed at a much older audience – aged from 60 to 80 – who might well be finding it harder to cope on their own in their current home and who would appreciate having a practical, well-equipped apartment where 24-hour assistance is available.

These retirement properties have been designed with older people in mind, containing easy-to-use appliances and a series of communal areas such as an owners' lounge and a restaurant. The tone of voice I've adopted tries to reflect the greater formality that older people tend to prefer and treats them with a courtesy and respect that I felt they would appreciate.

For example, I would not address anyone over the age of 60 in a personalised letter by their first name as that is likely to appear far too familiar, and it's really not a good idea to start off any correspondence by offending the recipient.

The second is a direct-mail leaflet aimed at an audience of trendy young professionals – aged between 25 and 35 – who currently work in London and who are either renting property in an expensive central location or on the outskirts of the city. We believe they might now be looking to buy a home of their own and we want to persuade them that they'll get much better value for money by moving outside Greater London.

The tone of voice I've used is cheeky and irreverent and reflects the more informal style of conversation that a younger crowd is likely to appreciate. It doesn't take itself too seriously and is quite tongue-in-cheek, but I hope it manages to get across the idea of how much more space – and what a better quality of life – you could enjoy if you bought a less expensive home within commuting distance of your place of work.

Dear [Mr/Mrs Personalised]

Thank you for the previous interest you have shown in our Retirement Living apartments at [site name]. I would like to take this opportunity to find out if you are indeed still interested in purchasing one of our new homes?

The reason I ask is that Bovis Homes currently have some very attractive spring offers that could save you a considerable sum of money. For example, right now when you buy one of our elegant apartments, we will arrange to pay for your Stamp Duty. Moreover, there will be no service charge for two years.

Our apartments represent a fresh approach to retirement living that allows owners to enjoy a secure and independent lifestyle with the reassurance of 24 hour support should you ever need it.

Just to remind you of the main benefits of our apartments at [site name] we can assure you that these homes are built to the highest standards and include a great number of attractive features.

For example, there is a convenient en suite to the main bedroom in most of our two bedroom apartments, while our modern fitted kitchens contain a complete range of practical appliances including a handy washer/dryer.

The comfortable sitting rooms offer you a feature fireplace, while the bedrooms also contain spacious fitted wardrobes. These homes also provide private parking plus you have the added benefit of attractive communal areas, including beautiful landscaped gardens.

Do let us know if you would like a further opportunity to view these highly attractive and practical new apartments at [site name].

If you are still considering whether a Bovis Homes Retirement Living apartment is the right choice for you, may I invite you to obtain some further information, or even arrange another visit to [site name] to see for yourself all the advantages of these new homes?

Of course if your needs have already been met, please do take the time to tell us using the attached reply-paid coupon and I'll remove your name from our mailing list. Otherwise, I look forward to welcoming you very soon at [site name].

Yours sincerely

Elizabeth Curry

Elizabeth Curry – Sales Manager

PS - Remember, you can use the enclosed reply-paid coupon to let us know your wishes and to arrange an appointment to view our latest apartments.

Need more room to swing your pants?

How about a town house in Reigate?

Bit of a tight fit?

Homes in central London can cost an arm and a leg – plus there's rarely room to dry your pants let alone swing 'em.

That's why you need to **wise up** and find out how much more space you could afford by buying a brand new town house in Reigate.

These homes give you plenty of room for manoeuvre, with well-equipped kitchens, generous living rooms, bedrooms with luxury en suites, secure parking – plus your very own private garden.

You'll even find a fully functioning washer/dryer where you can reinvigorate your pants ready for their next outing!

C'mon, shake a leg and get on down to view some of the grooviest houses in town.

To book a viewing just call us on **0845 000 000** or visit us at Blanford Mews, Blackborough Road, Reigate, Surrey RH2 7DE

www.bovishomes.co.uk

Can you rely on market research? ▷ Adopting the right tone of voice

Despite the chapter heading, this isn't meant to be a master class covering all aspects of writing in the English language. I don't think I'm qualified to undertake such an immense task, but I do want to share a few ideas and correct some common errors. There are some silly mistakes that many writers make. I'm sure I'm guilty of a few myself – and I'm happy to stand corrected when someone shows me the error of my ways.

Left:
A delightfully original campaign from Colman's mustard that doesn't pull its punches when it comes to promoting their product to the meat-eaters who make up their target audience. The agency has even coined a new word that combines 'meaty' and 'delicious' – *meatylicious* – to describe the delights of eating meat when combined with Colman's products. The *Meatylicious* website is also great fun – helpfully redirecting vegetarians to the official vegetarian website.

Client: Colman's
Agency: Karmarama

So, I don't want to give you a strict sermon on what you are and aren't allowed to do. It's up to you to weigh up the arguments for good or supposedly correct usage and then stick to the official line – or choose to break the rules as you see fit. The important thing is to know what effect you're going to have on an audience if you do overturn some cherished literary conventions.

The bad news is that the English language isn't always consistent and you often have choices to make concerning spelling, punctuation and sentence structure. Which means you must decide on a style for a client and then apply it consistently.

The good news is that advertising copywriting does give you more freedom to experiment with language. But, do remember that any writing you produce has to communicate your ideas effectively to your audience. If they don't understand what you're saying, then your client has just lost a load of sales.

Knowing your audience △ **Mastering the language** △ Sharpening your style

No one is likely to choose words more carefully than a copywriter. Which is presumably why most copywriters love dictionaries and spend a great deal of time poring over the words in their pages, observing their playful shades of meaning, delighting in their sensual forms and uncovering their rich and fascinating origins.

By using a dictionary that provides examples of words employed in a variety of contexts you can gain a much better sense of the subtle nuances which exist within words. By referring to a word's history and seeing how it has been used over generations you can build up a much better understanding of a word's associated meanings.

Even if it's only to confirm a word's spelling, a printed dictionary is likely to be your best and quickest ally, far simpler in most cases than having to log-on and gain your information from a digital source. Some people are in love with technology even if it involves more time, effort and frustration.

Books, including dictionaries, are going to retain their form for many years because they're so practical and convenient. There's no need for a power supply, an efficient computer, or a reliable Internet connection.

You can just pick up a book and turn its pages. You can read it in bed, on the beach – or even, if you must, on the toilet. And if it's a dictionary, you have the joy of discovering even more words and their meanings as you find yourself being distracted from your original search when your eye is taken by some other remarkable word.

Which is why my *Oxford Dictionary of English* is always on or by my desk so I can frequently refer to it in the course of my reading and writing. How else do you expect me to understand and have the temerity to use a word like 'fulminate', or indeed 'temerity'?

However, it does pay to keep your dictionary up-to-date. New words, and new meanings for words, enter the language all the time. English is constantly evolving and you need to understand how the language is currently being used if you wish to create topical advertising.

You also need to be aware of how people of all ages speak and write English by listening carefully to conversations, tuning in to television and radio shows and reading as widely as you can – from magazines to novels, from comic books to product packaging. You'll soon discover that, while there are obviously going to be broad overlaps in meaning, each age group and audience will have different ways of using language and their own specialised vocabulary.

Mastering the language

Copywriters are always weighing up the subtle variations in the meanings of words as we seek to control and direct our sentences to conjure up the correct mood and convey the right information.

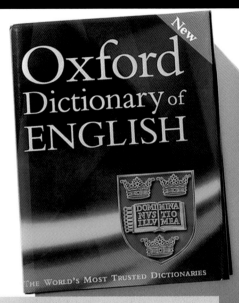

Right and below:
A good dictionary is worth its weight in words. Copywriters use their pens to earn pence so it pays to have a reference tool you can rely on to confirm the spellings, multiple meanings and generally accepted uses of words.

Word-check

Nuance – I didn't think I'd need to provide this definition but many of my first year students recently claimed they'd never heard the word before.

So, just in case you share their verbal innocence, the word 'nuance' has been borrowed from French and means 'any subtle difference in meaning or expression'.

It's a great word for indicating or suggesting very subtle and evocative differences – those minute shades of meaning that are sometimes distinct and yet at other times overlap.

There's almost a sense of taste or smell to the word as if you're sniffing the air to pick up a subtle and sensitive alteration in flavour or scent.

Improving your language skills △ Technical assistance

The thesaurus is extinct

Don't waste your time burying your nose in the decaying carcass of that old dinosaur, the thesaurus. Someone did buy me one as a present when I started out in advertising. It was a kind thought but the thesaurus has since sat gathering dust on my bookshelves looking at me mournfully as only a beast on the edge of extinction can manage.

There's precious little point in looking for alternative words – or synonyms – if you don't already have them to hand in your head. Which is where you'll have a better understanding of their meaning, their weight and where they will fall most fittingly into your text.

Apart from the fact that you might risk using a word whose meaning you don't fully understand, or be tempted to replace a simple word with a complicated one, you might be making the mistake of only changing one word when you really need to adjust the whole shape and form of a paragraph or page.

If a word isn't working, you might need to restructure your sentence, rewrite an entire paragraph, or reconstruct the whole page to make the words flow more smoothly and make your meaning more comprehensible. And you really shouldn't be afraid of such major changes.

But just in case you're feeling nervous about making such wholesale alterations to your text because you're not sure how it's going to turn out, I'll give you a practical tip: use your word-processing editing tools to copy and save the section you're working on.

Either save the troublesome section in another Word document or simply paste it above or below the section that you're about to perform open-heart surgery upon. Then if all goes wrong and the patient dies, you can always revert to your previous version, and start the procedure all over again.

This method also allows you to pick out a choice phrase or maybe a key word and save it for use in your new and improved version. In other words you're using your original section of text as a quarry for reclaimed material.

Above:
Home sweet home? What kind of property do you live in and how does it make you feel? While the wealthy might enjoy stately homes and mansions, the world's poor people can be reduced to living in hovels within shanty towns and ghettos. There's a great deal of emotion and meaning invested in that single word 'home'.

Now it's your turn

Test your power of synonyms. I made a bold claim that you shouldn't rely on a thesaurus to find alternative words or expressions. So now I'll set you a personal challenge.

Try coming up with your own list of parallel, associated or similar-meaning words and phrases for the following terms without referring to a dictionary, thesaurus or any other reference tool. I know that some of these are going to prove tougher than others.

Big	**Strength**	**Bright**
Sexy	**Reliable**	**Fashion**
Home	**Pleasure**	**Creativity**

Think of the various contexts in which you might use such words. Also, take the time to review your alternative words and phrases to establish how their meanings vary in subtle and significant ways from the original word.

For example, how does the word 'home' differ from the word 'house'? Which word carries more emotional associations – and what are those associations?

Improving your language skills △ Technical assistance

Over the past 20 years, some of the greatest improvements for copywriters have been the advances in word-processing power and the ready availability of PCs and Apple Macs – together with the digital technology of the Internet that allows rapid e-mail communication and online research.

But to concentrate on the power of word-processing; for many years now it's been so easy to adapt and modify your text, to shift sections about, to try out new phrases, to adjust wording and change the order of your paragraphs, etc. And that flexibility is an important consideration when you're a copywriter because we're forever changing our minds – and changing our text.

In our quest for best expression we seem to be endlessly fine-tuning our language and shifting phrases around – all in a bid to improve the style and flow of our copy. And of course, there's never enough time when you have a deadline looming. (Lucy, when did you say I had to finish this book?)

Computers and their word-processing programs offer a variety of tools that can help reduce errors, including a basic spell-check function – although it's best not to rely on it too much. First you have to set it to British or American English (which some UK writers fail to do, leaving it on the US default) and then you need to check your own copy for any errors that the system hasn't, or can't, pick up.

For example, if your mistake spells another word then no warning message of red underlining will appear. Maybe you wanted to write 'bump in the road', but if you accidentally type 'bum in the road', well, so be it; the computer recognises the word 'bum' and thinks you meant to write it.

And just a word of warning to try and prevent Anglo-American confusion: in UK English a bum is a bottom rather than a hobo or tramp, while in North American English a bottom is a fanny. Oh dear, there's another embarrassing difference in trans-Atlantic meaning.

Re-reading your copy also gives you a further chance to uncover any awkward phrasing and amend your text accordingly. It helps to read your copy out loud or, if people start giving you funny looks, at least try to hear how it sounds in your head. Hearing it that way gives you a much better impression of how well the copy flows and whether any clumsy expressions need to be adjusted.

Along the way, you might also spot some grammatical errors or repeated repeated words – which can often happen when you've been fiddling about with your cut-and-paste tool and moving copy around your document.

I don't like the idea of rules in writing, but here's a rule for you. Check your work and then re-check your work for errors. Ideally, get someone else to check your writing as well – although that luxury isn't always available.

Word-check

Program – if you're a writer of UK English, then the only time you'll spell this word as program (rather than programme) is when you're referring to computer programs.

The fact that so much hi-tech computer technology has been developed in the USA (despite Alan Turing's sterling efforts for the UK) has led to this spelling of the word being adopted for all computer applications.

This anomaly can lead to some bizarre parallel appearances in promotional material such as when a UK company offers a 'Programme of seminars on database management programs'.

The same distinction usually applies to the UK word 'disc' versus the North American 'disk', which is the preferred form for computer applications, such as 'hard disk'.

Above and below:
Computers and their word-processing software can supply the copywriter with a wide range of tools.

Improving your language skills △ Technical assistance △ Knowing the rules and when to break them

Spelling and its pitfalls

Spelling and punctuation in the English language might indeed be complicated but copywriters must take responsibility not only for the style but also the accuracy of their writing. Any errors you commit – or fail to pick up – will not only make you look foolish but can also prove very costly, especially when print is concerned.

An incorrect spelling in a headline on the front cover of an annual report which results in 10,000 copies having to be reprinted is going to cost a fortune – and probably your job. Chief Executives of large companies are not usually known for their sense of humour and benevolent reaction in the face of such incompetence.

To avoid such liability most agencies will ask clients to 'sign off' copy in adverts and brochures, but any failure to spot a mistake is still likely to lead to ill-feeling and the client/agency relationship is bound to suffer.

Then there's the added complication that some words can indeed be spelt – or spelled – in two different ways, so you have to choose your preference and stick to it. 'Focused' or 'focussed'? Both are correct, so the choice is yours – or your clients'.

In fact, the English language is a real oddity; a right royal mongrel of accumulated words from various old and new languages with Anglo-Saxon – an early Germanic language – supplemented by Latin, Greek, French and many other imported foreign terms as we were in turn invaded or went off and invaded other lands.

The result of all this promiscuous interaction is a rich vocabulary and a host of weird and inconsistent spellings. Bill Bryson in his entertaining book on the English language, *Mother Tongue*, provides a brief challenge for anyone who thinks they can spell well.

Just as a quick test, see if you can tell which of the following words are mispelled.

supercede	*rhythym*
conceed	*opthalmologist*
procede	*diptheria*
idiosyncracy	*anamoly*
concensus	*afficianado*
accomodate	*caesarian*
impressario	*grafitti*

In fact, they all are. So was misspelled *at the end of the preceeding paragraph. So was* preceding *just there. I'm sorry, I'll stop. But I trust you get the point that English can be a maddeningly difficult language to spell correctly.*

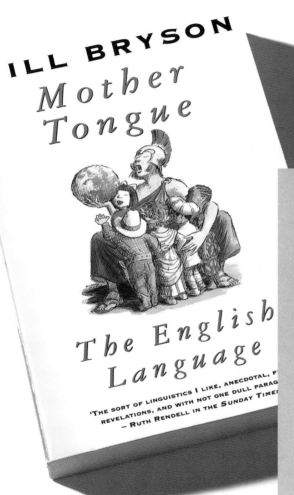

Word-check

Adviser or **advisor** – here's another example of an alternative spelling and one that often crops up in financial services advertising.

Somehow, to my eyes and ears, 'advisor' looks and sounds more 'hard sell', so I tend to prefer 'adviser'.

'Adviser' seems to suggest a less pushy and more helpful person who will offer you friendly and trustworthy advice.

Whereas an 'advisor' would appear much more likely to lock you in a room and spend three hours telling you why you must buy this very expensive time-share apartment right next to the fish market.

Spelling and punctuation might be complicated but copywriters have a duty to learn how to play their instrument if they wish to ply their trade.

Improving your language skills △ Technical assistance △ Knowing the rules and when to break them

Advertising copywriters are often accused of using incorrect English and breaking grammatical rules. Thankfully these are often quite minor offences that are generally permitted by the language police – as long as you're carrying your poetic licence.

In press and poster ads we do like to use short, crisp sentences. Like this. Just to make a point. And purists will tell you that such a construction is technically not a sentence because it doesn't contain a verb and a subject. And you know what? We just don't care. Because we're rebels. Rebels without a clause.

It's a shame that grammar and its close analysis can appear so exceedingly dull. Some of the pedants who push it seem intent on making their subject so dreary that the excitement and energy of language gets lost within their musty paragraphs.

And yet, you do need to develop a basic understanding of how language works and how it can best be put together to make your writing both personal and immediate. Perhaps the only way of achieving a profound and sincere appreciation of language is to read widely and judge for yourself what sounds right and works best.

Yes, it probably is useful to know about basic sentence structure, and similarly it might help to convince people of your writing abilities if you can recognise a noun, a verb, an adjective, an adverb and maybe even a pronoun and a preposition. But beyond that, I don't think copywriters need to have a more detailed knowledge of grammatical terminology.

I have learned what a 'gerund' is – and it's not a small furry animal that resides in warm countries. It's a verb form that acts as a noun: 'Her **acting** ran the whole gamut of emotions from A to B' (to paraphrase Dorothy Parker's review of a Katharine Hepburn opening night) but I wouldn't say this knowledge has improved my writing ability in any discernible way.

Moreover I don't know what an 'ablative disjunctive phrase' is, presumably because it's a term I've just made up. Sorry, I just wanted to demonstrate that most of us are scared of grammar and confused by its complex terminology. The point I'm trying to make is that you don't have to possess a comprehensive knowledge of grammatical terms – or rhetorical devices – to be able to write well.

By all means get yourself a style guide and learn when to use initial capital letters on South England but not on southern England, when to write 10 or spell it out as ten, etc. There are many technical details and odd matters of accepted usage that you'll need to confirm during your writing career so having such a resource to hand is likely to come in very useful.

Above:
Man's faithful and playful friend
or a highly trained killer?
A symbol of loyal devotion and
hard work or a soppy flea-ridden
beast with embarrassing
flatulence? A dog can represent
so many different things.

While many of us might struggle to identify obscure grammatical forms, that should not prevent us from writing well and expressing ourselves with power and authority.

Word-check

Denotation and **connotation** – some commentators make a distinction between what a word 'denotes' at a literal level and what it 'connotes' at a symbolic level. For example, the word 'dog' supposedly *denotes* or represents the four-legged domesticated animal with a love of lamp posts, while the word 'dog' *connotes* 'loyalty' – or whatever value the theorist wishes to attach.

Apart from the fact that 'denote' and 'connote' are rather pretentious verbs to explain simple concepts, this approach seems to overlook the fascinating truth that words can signify many things at the same time. Meanwhile their meaning is shaped by their context because words are strongly influenced by the other words and images that surround them – and that is what the copywriter seeks to control.

In some circumstances the word 'dog' might indeed signify or suggest loyalty, but it can also be an indicator of domesticity or savagery, lethargy or vitality, high spirits or depression, etc. Dogs have been used at different times in advertising campaigns to suggest bad breath and wall paint, so it's up to you how you shape your meanings.

Technical assistance △ Knowing the rules and when to break them

Punctilious about punctuation

Try not to be scared of punctuation: all those sharp dots and threatening squiggles. The whole point of punctuation is to enable you to express your meaning more clearly – and to help the people who are reading your writing, do so in the way you want it to be read.

In most instances punctuation is there to tell the reader when to pause – and how long to pause. No two writers will use exactly the same punctuation, with one perhaps choosing to break up phrases with more commas than another. The important thing is to use punctuation to help get your messages across quickly and with clarity.

Colons, semicolons and dashes

As an advertising copywriter, I've slipped into the habit of the running dash. Cutting a dash with your punctuation might be frowned upon in some literary circles – but it can be a useful device that keeps your copy flowing rather than interrupting it with abrupt colons and stifling semicolons.

Colons are useful for introducing a list, expanding on a statement or establishing parallel ideas – while semicolons are useful if you want to make those cute little smiley faces in e-mails and text messages ;).

Only kidding; the semicolon is meant to indicate a weightier pause than a comma and is typically used between clauses that might have been separate sentences: 'The sky cleared; the children played'. However, it's equally possible to write this line in different ways, including as two separate sentences, divided with a colon, or more loosely linked with a comma.

Given the confusion and doubt that surrounds the use of these punctuation marks, it's not surprising that many people are falling back on using just commas and full stops with the occasional long dash.

However, despite the frequency with which the running dash is beginning to appear, it's remarkable how many writers, artworkers and typographers don't know where to find it on their keyboard. All too often a measly hyphen is used instead of that sweeping and dashing dash.

To type a long dash on my Apple Mac you need to hold down the 'alt' key and press the 'hyphen' key – whereupon, lo and behold, a smart long dash appears. (Good typographers even distinguish between the en-dash and the em-dash as opposed to the hyphen and use them appropriately.)

Typographical tip – don't type two spaces after a full stop and before the next sentence, just one. I know typists were often taught to do this, but it drives artworkers crazy since they have to go through your text and remove those extra spaces before they can fit your copy into their artwork.

Below:
The surprising popularity of Lynne Truss's exploration of punctuation proved that many people were indeed concerned enough about the subject to want to learn more – or at least worried enough to have their concerns and prejudices reinforced.

Eats ҉ Shoots
& 🐼 Leaves

The Zero Tolerance
Approach to Punctuation
!

LYNNE TRUSS

When hyphens stray

Hyphens appear to be an endangered species and yet, once again, they're a useful device for clarifying your meaning which can otherwise become unhinged. (Did you see what I did there?)

Lynne Truss in her surprising best-seller, *Eats, Shoots and Leaves*, which dealt at some length with matters of punctuation gives a traditional example of how the absence of hyphens can sometimes lead to confusion. Is a 'pickled herring seller' a seller of pickled-herrings or has the herring-seller been pickled?

Some smarty-pants did subsequently point out that Lynne Truss had fallen down on her own use of the hyphen by managing to miss it out of the subtitle of her book, *The Zero Tolerance Approach to Punctuation*, where it should have appeared as *Zero-Tolerance Approach*. I tell you, it's tough getting it right when you write.

A lack of hyphens confused me when I read a local NHS Primary Care Trust leaflet that provided details of a 'Well Baby Drop In Clinic'. At first glance this looked like a tabloid headline announcing the bizarre and dangerous practice of dropping babies in wells at clinics or, alternatively, a sad decline in healthy babies visiting clinics. I suppose they meant a 'drop-in clinic'.

Above:
Fused or confused? The shop sign should read 'open every day' which is then convenient for your 'everyday' shopping needs. Meanwhile, a fitness club is using a clever play on words when they choose to emphasise 'every body' rather than the expected 'everybody'.

Presumably the current lack of hyphens is due to the sheer confusion about when it is appropriate to use them. They're simply being left off in the mistaken belief that, if you don't put them in, you can't possibly be wrong.

Mastering the language

When words collide

Why some terms should be squashed together while others remain chastely apart also remains a bit of a mystery. We accept 'into' but not 'upto'; we happily embrace 'yesterday' but wouldn't countenance 'nextweek' – well, not yet anyway (rather than 'any way' in this context).

Some people have even taken to writing 'alot', rather than 'a lot', possibly confusing it with the verb 'to allot', meaning to share out, to apportion (or to dig your council-owned vegetable patch?).

Once again we're dealing with the fact that the English language is not set in all its ways and we have choices to make. For example, the term 'fundraising' can also be written as 'fund-raising' and 'fund raising'. It isn't a matter of one form being correct while the others are wrong. It's more a question of individual style and accepted usage. Personally, I think that the word 'fundraising' looks distinctly odd without a hyphen and yet it seems we're stuck with this popular usage which makes it appear as if we're intent on 'draising' some 'fun'.

Clients and their agencies simply have to agree on what style they're going to follow and then stick to it. For writers who are new to a company, it helps if there's a reliable style guide that resolves these issues and gives you clear guidance on which form of words and phrases you're meant to use.

domainnames.com

The process of phrases being crushed together has been hastened by the development of Internet domain names that won't permit any spaces, which can also lead to confusion.

A website that offers a review of pop music from the 1960s might think twice about calling itself: www.sixtieshits.com. (In fact, the last time I looked some Dutch guy was trying to sell this name, presumably not realising that it looked, well, a bit shitty – or, to use that traditional Dutch term, like a load of old poppycock.)

Also, although it's a fine website for a splendid company, I had some slight concerns about the title 'the fitness team' when its domain name ended up looking like it ended in 'steam': 'thefitnessteam'. At least when you write such domain names in marketing material you can use initial capital letters or embolden one of the words to make them easier to read, for example, TheFitnessTeam or the**fitness**team.

There are some terms whose position in a sentence dictates whether they should be together or apart. For example, *sometimes* it's appropriate to fuse a phrase – and there are *some times* when it's not.

Sins of omission and possession

How come so many people don't know where to stick their apostrophes? Even writers for publishing companies apparently have to be issued with a guide telling us where and when to use *its* as opposed to *it's* – which is presumably an indictment of our educational system, or perhaps just an indication of the calibre of us writers what is writing these days.

I suppose it goes back to the fact that much of our English language isn't necessarily logical, but is instead standardised usage that we simply have to learn. So, let's have a quick lesson and gain some guidelines. Get these basics wrong and you can look like a right idiot.

The apostrophe is used to indicate missing letters

Apostrophes pop up where words have been pushed together to indicate how we speak, for example, *I'll*, *we'll*, *can't*, *won't*, *shan't*, *wouldn't*, etc. This kind of informal written language is very common in advertising copy where we're usually trying to be personal and immediate. I suppose we're generally trying to write as we speak, or at least trying to give that impression.

You can tell from this list that the apostrophe isn't always placed where you might expect it. '*Shall not*' is abbreviated to '*shan't*' where the apostrophe fills in for the 'o' in 'not' but the double 'l' from 'shall' is simply missing. The word '*won't*' is an odd contraction of 'will not' and yet that's how we say it.

Then there are further expressions such as *let's*, *you're* and *they're* where again two words have been 'elided' together as in speech, standing for: *let us*, *you are* and *they are*. However, confusion can arise here since there are other words with different meanings that sound just like these abbreviated constructions: *lets*, *your*, *there* and *their*, so you'll need to check carefully exactly what you've written.

One well-known high street shop had some giant posters put up in their windows featuring the massive headline 'Your the star'. Not the star of spelling, obviously. You're kidding? No, I'm not, so it pays to check you're work. Oh dear, now I'm doing it.

The apostrophe is used when you're being possessive

Now for the possessive form of words and where to plonk that tricky apostrophe. You use an apostrophe at the end of a word, usually with an accompanying 's', to indicate that the items which follow belong to that object, for example, *the chair's legs*. You can see they belong to the chair when you turn the phrase round and say *the legs of the chair*. If there are many chairs then you have to use the plural form and place the apostrophe after the final 's', *the chairs' legs* or, in other words these are *the legs of the chairs*.

It can be confusing when the singular form of the word already ends in an 's' but the general rule is to spell it as you would say it. If you want to refer to the wheels of the bus, then you'd say and write *the bus's wheels*. Again, if there were many buses, then they would be *the buses' wheels*, ie *the wheels of the buses* when we reverse the order of the phrase.

Further confusion can arise when the word not only ends in an 's' but sounds as if you wouldn't say the extra possessive 's'. So, you might see a sign for *St James' Street* in one town and *St James's Street* in another. It all depends on how you've chosen to pronounce this street name. Some councils wouldn't even bother with a possessive 's' and simply call it *St James Street*. Ho hum.

When it comes to the English language '*it's* time to embrace *its* illogicality'.

Now for that common error: *its* versus *it's*, Having said that the apostrophe 's' form is used to indicate possession, this guideline does not apply to 'its' where the possessive pronoun remains firmly free of apostrophes.

A good way of remembering this rule is to think of those possessive equivalents, *his* and *hers* which are also pronouns that don't have apostrophes: *Oh dear this table is wobbly. Its legs are broken*. If you think of the table as a person or an animal and substitute the word *its* with *his – His legs are broken* – you might just find it easier to remember the correct spelling.

It will also help you remember the difference in use of *its* and *it's* if you know that the **only** time you're meant to see *it's* is when the apostrophe is being used to indicate the missing letters in the term *it is* or *it has*. Don't fight it. Just accept it.

Technical assistance ▷ Knowing the rules and when to break them

And why not?

There are some people who mistakenly believe that you should never start a sentence with an 'And' or a 'But'. And yet, why not? You may well ask, for there is no grammatical rule against such a sentence structure.

This old prejudice appears to be instilled within the susceptible minds of small children by primary school teachers who tell their innocent charges – formerly on pain of slapped legs – never to commence a sentence with the word 'And'. And then they slap the same injunction on the word 'But'.

I'm sure it must be annoying for such teachers to face an endless barrage of staccato sentences in response to the request, 'Now children, I want you to write about what you did this weekend'.

Little Connor – or his sister Chardonnay – obliges:

This weekend Mummy and Daddy
took me to the seaside.
And then we played in the sea.
And after that we had ice cream.
And then we went to the fairground.
And then I had candyfloss.
And as a treat we all went on the dodgems.
And then I was sick.

Rather than impose a total ban, these early arbiters of style should be teaching moderation. After all, for as long as the English language has been set down in written form, 'And' and 'But' have performed their duty at the beginning of sentences.

From Middle English verse throughout King James's Bible (the Authorised Version no less) and on through the works of Charles Dickens to the modern era, writers of the English language have continued to adopt this practice.

To quote the Good Book (Gen. 39: 7, 8):

And it came to pass after these things,
that his master's wife cast her eyes
upon Joseph; and she said, Lie with me.
But he refused…

Or, here's a section from *Oliver Twist* following the brutal murder of Nancy at the hands of Bill Sykes. See how the shock and immediacy of the moment is conveyed through the initial use of that small yet highly significant word 'And':

And there was the body – mere flesh
and blood, no more – but such flesh, and
so much blood!

And there are a great deal more modern examples. But perhaps I've made my point? Unfortunately, as commercial copywriters, we sometimes have to bow to client pressure, but I reserve the right to point out that my usage is correct. Even if I do overuse this device!

Left and below:
Talking of school rules, secondary school children were the audience for this unusual guide to growing up which makes striking use of a junior *Janet and John* or *Ladybird* books style of illustration and typography. These so called *Bee Books* deal with some very senior issues such as peer pressure, sexual ignorance and malicious gossip. Innocence and experience combine in one clever treatment that is sure to grab attention and increase awareness.

Agency: Guy Robertson Partnership
Client: NHS Glasgow
Copywriter: Martin Cross
Art Director: Mark Williams
Illustrator: Alan McGowan

20

Next day after games the girls in her class tease her.
"Haven't you shagged Tam yet?" asks Shona.
Kirsty shakes her head.

key word   tease

38

Tam and Kirsty walk through the park.
They see Anne-Marie sitting on the roundabout on her own.
She's holding an empty bottle and she's covered in her own vomit.

To infinitive and beyond

Here we have another old favourite that enrages certain people: the split infinitive. Once again, there's no rule that governs where you should stick your adverb in relation to the infinitive form of a verb, which in English is the basic construction 'to go', 'to throw', 'to complain', 'to fulminate', etc.

According to some old-fashioned types, since the Latin form can't be split (not surprising really since it consists of only one word in that dead language: *porter*: to carry, etc) they believe the English form shouldn't be split either. In other words, they'd rather see and hear 'to complain needlessly' than 'to needlessly complain'.

Such people seem to make up the majority of regular complainants to BBC Radio 4 and they're the same people who must shudder every time the opening credits to Star Trek come up and Captain Kirk's voice-over solemnly intones, '…to boldly go where no man has gone before'.

Sometimes the split infinitive, where the adverb appears in the middle, does sound slightly odd but similarly you can produce some ill-sounding alternatives when you don't split it. Does it really sound better to say 'to go boldly' rather than 'to boldly go' – or does it sound clumsy and awkward?

Feel free to split your infinitives when it sounds better but be aware that you're going to meet with disapproval from some quarters and, once again, you might need to bow to public prejudice.

Stick to your guns and you might find that you've upset some members of your audience who will be so annoyed at your supposed misuse of English that they refuse to think well of your advertising message. Can you and your client afford to upset so many people?

Above:
Boldly splitting infinitives across the universe, Captain Kirk managed to annoy fuddy-duddies back home who had nothing better to drearily do than to needlessly complain.

Image courtesy of Paramount Television/ The Kobal Collection

Being right isn't always enough. If sufficient people – and particularly your clients – object to a certain usage then you probably need to gracefully give in to their misapplied pressure.

Word-check

Fulminate – If you're not already familiar with the term, I'm going to leave you to look that one up. (To make it easier for you there is a definition from the *Oxford Dictionary of English* back on page 63.) And yet, I wouldn't recommend using obscure words in your advertising unless it's for a specialist audience who will be sure to understand your terminology.

That well-known copywriter and advertising man, David Ogilvy, generally promoted the use of simple and factual language but, like many wordsmiths, he couldn't always resist the opportunity to stick an unusual word in his copy. Defending his use of long copy for the famous 'noisy clock' ad for Rolls-Royce he explained:

In the last paragraph I wrote, 'People who feel diffident about driving a Rolls-Royce can buy a Bentley.' Judging from the number of motorists who picked up the word 'diffident' and bandied it about, I concluded that the advert was thoroughly read.

However, I wonder just how many of the people supposedly using this relatively unusual word were truly confident of its meaning?

Technical assistance ▷ Knowing the rules and when to break them

Granny Smiths.

What's the difference between ours and our competitors'?

Not much really.

They're the same quality as Waitrose.

And the same price as Asda.

TESCO | Every little helps

Readers want to be entertained
while they're being informed:
if you can engage their interest
with wit and style, they're more likely
to respond to your advertising with
warmth and affection.

As you know by now, advertising
takes many forms and copywriting
is used to help generate a vast range
of promotional material, covering
posters, press ads, mailpacks, sales
brochures, websites, TV commercials,
radio ads – and so much more.

The fact that you have to adjust your style –
and often your technique – when you write
for these different media forms suggests
that copywriters have to be cunning
craftspeople, carefully shaping their copy
to fit their medium and suit their audience.

Personally I view copywriting as an alliance
between an art and a craft. I certainly
don't believe there's an absolute science
to copywriting. That's why I'm wary of
hard-sell pamphlets that offer to teach you
some such nonsense as 'The 10 strongest
words in the English language, each
guaranteed to boost your sales by 100%'.
Still, I suppose sufficient people are
suitably gullible and keen to find quick
and easy solutions: perhaps I should
publish just such a guide?

If only it were that easy to create irresistible
advertising. Copywriters would have a rigid
set of scientific rules to follow. Following
this practical guide, we'd simply have to
put such words as 'new' and 'amazing' into
our text and suddenly we'd have a piece
of dynamic and successful copy. Another
job well done: let's all go to the pub.

Well, I'm sorry to say that there are no such
simple scientific techniques. You also
have to accept that what worked today
won't necessarily have the same effect
tomorrow. People get used to certain
approaches and become immune to
them, like pesky mosquitoes thwarting
the latest pesticide.

Our customers often want something
that looks fresh and different to tickle
their interests, move their imaginations
and loosen their wallets.

Left:
Tesco have adopted a witty style
of wordplay allied to strong
yet simple imagery in their
advertising. It's good to see
words being used so well,
and with such powerful results.

Client: Tesco
Agency: Lowe London

Mastering the language △ **Sharpening your style** △ Rules and restrictions

If copywriting isn't exactly a science, am I allowed to claim copywriting as an art? Well, I believe all language, including advertising language, can be poetical and therefore has the potential for artistic merit.

I'm not saying that the text for every advert is beautiful but I do see copywriting as a form of artistic expression. There also needs to be a natural rhythm to language for it to sound right – and for it to achieve suitable impact.

In fact, all the techniques of the poet are available to the copywriter if you are able to harness them: rhythm, rhyme, alliteration, assonance, metaphor, simile, onomatopoeia, litotes, zeugma, etc.

OK, so we don't necessarily have to worry about obscure Greek-sounding names for these tricks of the writing trade but that doesn't stop you using them every day of your life, even when you talk to your friends, colleagues and family.

Literary devices are merely ways of enlivening your language and making your conversation and writing more colourful and entertaining. It's an everyday expression, but which sounds more immediate and dynamic: 'Put the kettle on. I'm dying for a cuppa.' or 'Please fill the electric kettle with water and switch it on. I'm feeling thirsty and would appreciate a cup of tea.'?

The thoughts of other copywriters

Just to broaden the debate, Adrian Crane at the agency Factor 3 offers the following thoughts on advertising copywriting where he plays down the purely artistic in favour of commercial creativity. The critical point made here is not to lose sight of the overriding business objectives of your advertising:

Advertising is a creative endeavour but it is not an art. An American Art Director once described it as the bastard art of an imprecise science. It serves a purely commercial purpose whose role is (through engagement, entertainment, informing) to sell – it is simply what you do when you can't be there to sell in person. So write to satisfy the bottom line not your own literary ambitions.

Every piece of communication has a tone-of-voice, a personality, which in marketing, shouldn't be the writer's. The personality should echo the brand and the tone should be appropriate to the medium and the audience. Marketing copy is a company speaking not you writing.

Sharpening your style

Lead your country to glory with UEFA EURO 2004™

Above:
Simple and direct in style.
An atmospheric shot of the
famous Brazilian football player,
Ronaldinho, relaxing on the
beach at Rio de Janeiro.
Naturally, his national team
aren't eligible to play in the
European contest, so his
individual artistry will be absent,
but in this computer game
version, *you* can be playing.
The image and text put you
on the same level as one of
the world's greatest footballers.

Client: EA SPORTS: Euro 2004
Agency: OWN+P
Creative Director: Bruce Crouch
Copywriter: Neil Cook
Art Director: Jason Fairclough

**Dull pictures and dreary words
lack impact. Make your advertising
more interesting by using language
and imagery that grabs and holds
the reader's attention.**

The art and craft of copywriting △ Generating creative ideas

Learn to appreciate writing for its quality and cadences. Acquire the ability to assess an item of text for the effects it achieves, and try to understand just how those dramatic effects have been created.

Developing a love of language

As a cynical yet romantic copywriter I believe you must love language in all its forms. And if you love language, you will be a reader – otherwise where else are you going to draw your inspiration from and so improve your range? Whether it's a classic novel, a cheap thriller or the back of a cornflake packet, you will read avidly. You simply can't help yourself.

Unless you already have, or can develop, a love of language then, I'm sorry, but you're really not cut out for a career as a copywriter. I don't want to put you off, but an interest in your native language combined with a love of reading and a natural desire to analyse words and phrases are key requirements for professional writers.

After all, you can learn a great deal about writing styles when you discover how other people have written.

So, if you're not alive to the possibilities of language, if you don't enjoy playing with words, shifting phrases to produce the right effect and create subtle shades of meaning, then copywriting isn't for you.

I hope I haven't just alienated a large number of my own readers. Maybe there are some would-be copywriters out there who don't currently read very much but who will be inspired by my words to read more books, magazines, articles – and cereal boxes. Perhaps you can also be persuaded to listen to more TV scripts and radio broadcasts. It all helps to build up a broad vocabulary and a deeper understanding of a wide variety of styles.

I promise you'll be rewarded, especially if in the process of further reading and listening, you can develop your sensitivity to the English language in all its written and spoken forms.

Think about the tone of voice and the kind of vocabulary. Are they appropriate for the intended audience? How colourful is the language and what kind of poetical or literary effects have been employed? In your opinion, is it too complicated, too flowery, or perhaps even too simple for this particular audience?

Sharpening your style

Finest Mozzarella di Bufala.

Camembert de Normandie.

And Brie de Meaux.

Now available...

Just past les Triangles
de Dairylea.

Subject to availability at selected UK stores. Serving suggestion.

TESCO | *Every little helps*

Above:
It's fun to play with language
and engage your audience with
clever copy. Here's one more in
the series of great ads produced
for Tesco, this time playing
on the notion of Italian and
French cheeses.

Client: Tesco
Agency: Lowe London

The art and craft of copywriting △ Generating creative ideas

Advertising language as heightened communication

Just to demonstrate a few of the techniques that copywriters use, let's have a look at some examples of advertising copy that apply rhyme, alliteration, repetition and other literary devices to good effect. On the next spread I'm going to set you an exercise to test your ability to shape short copy. That's why I want to concentrate here on brief, effective headlines and punchy, memorable straplines.

As these posters for OXY spot cream prove, the use of dramatic illustration – in this case, reflecting a colourful comic-book style – can make a huge impact in terms of getting your adverts noticed.

Here the images demonstrate an idealised *before* and *after* where the medicated skin cream has healed spots while the headlines reinforce the effectiveness of this process by using short rhyming lines and trendy vocabulary: from 'rough to ruff' and from 'zitty to pretty'. Note how the choice of words has been heavily influenced by North American teen-talk: 'buff', 'zitty'; both words that have now entered UK English usage thanks to our exposure to 'movies' and 'TV shows' from the USA.

(The American English terms 'movies' and 'TV shows' are so imbedded in UK English vocabulary that they no longer really merit being distinguished as unusual, although as recently as a generation ago the terms 'films' and 'TV programmes' would have been more standard expressions.)

This use of rhyme in advertising is very popular, and no wonder, since it is a neat and simple method that allows you to emphasise points in a memorable way.

From an early age we are taught to spot similarities between sounds and as children we enjoy rhyming songs and nursery rhymes. Then, as we grow older, we still like traditional forms of poetry and popular music where 'love and marriage' go together 'like a horse and carriage', or where the phrase 'he was a skater boy' is followed by, 'I said see you later boy'.

Perhaps the essence of the copywriter's art can be found in straplines where many effective poetical techniques are pressed into use to create short phrases that are easy to remember and which serve to shape and reinforce our perception of a particular product or brand.

Effective design is even more important than clever headlines when it comes to grabbing attention, but ideally both elements will work in harmony to create maximum impact.

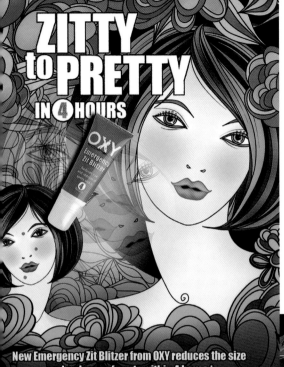

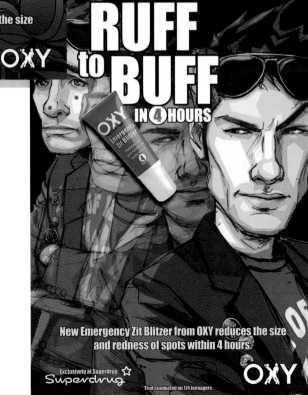

Left and below:
Bright, bold and colourful posters aimed at a young audience with retro-style comic-book illustrations demonstrate the transformation that this skin product promises: from spotty to hotty, or as the ads have it from 'ruff to buff' and from 'zitty to pretty'.

Client: Oxy
Agency: Ogilvy Healthworld

The art and craft of copywriting △ Generating creative ideas

Straplines say it with wit and style

Straplines, or what used to be called 'slogans', are popular as a simple way to summarise your brand and emphasise what it represents. Sitting at the foot of adverts or voiced at the end of a TV or radio ad, the strapline has become almost as important as the company name and logo and often sits alongside them to reinforce the brand and assert its individuality.

A strong strapline can last for many years, even decades, although there's been a recent tendency for some brands to adopt a fresh strapline every year, almost as a style guide to their seasonal campaigns. And so, for example, *The Lynx effect* was transformed into the less subtle and more overtly sexual *Spray more. Get more*. It's not always easy to tell if such a phrase is working as a headline or a strapline, since they can often become interchangeable.

The most effective straplines are those that are easy to remember and which relate directly to a product feature or benefit. It also helps if you can incorporate the company, product or brand name within the strapline, for example *Ariston and on and on*, *Go to work on an egg*, *Have a break, have a KitKat*, etc. Double-meanings and witty wordplays often appear in straplines: *The car in front is a Toyota*, or for Ford: *Everything we do is driven by you*.

Probably the best strapline in the world

Computer companies often try to inject their products with emotion such as Microsoft's *Where do you want to go today?* which is a clever line for a static PC. Meanwhile, Apple Mac – whose products I use and generally like – annoyed me with their illiterate *Think different*. It's an adverb you dolt. That should be *Think differently*. Still, I did say copywriters were allowed to bend the rules.

Over the years beer brands have had fun creating straplines that make some over-the-top claims but seem to get away with it by using tongue-in-cheek humour: *Heineken refreshes the parts other beers cannot reach* (subsequently abbreviated to *How refreshing. How Heineken*) and *Carlsberg – probably the best lager in the world*. Probably? Says who?

Some straplines seem ultra-modern in their clipped one word form: Budweiser *True*, Coca-Cola *Real*. This is not just short copy: it's minimalist copy that leaves you nowhere else to go. Such monosyllabic abbreviations, like the micro-mini skirt, suggest it's time for a change in fashions and, as hems descend, so phrases might well become that bit longer so we'll be able to make more of a statement.

Compare Coke's curt *Real* with that old 1970s fizzin' beauty in jive-jingle form from arch-rival Pepsi-Cola where you can almost feel the fizz in your throat:

LipSmackinThirstQuenchinAceTastin MotivatinGoodBuzzinCoolTalkinHighWalkin FastLivinEverGivinCoolFizzin Pepsi.

Now it's your turn

We've looked at a fair few straplines
so I hope you'll be suitably inspired
to try and create some of your own.

Now for the products: Reebok trainers,
Cadbury Dairy Milk chocolate,
London Pride ale, Marks & Spencer.
See if you can come up with a variety
of strapline options for each.

Rather than invent products I thought
I'd let you work on new straplines for all
these established brands.

That way, you'll be able to research their
current image and then develop suitable
new slogans that are appropriate for these
brands and which reflect their values.

Word-check

Logotype – now usually abbreviated
to 'logo' and originally used to define a
company or product name created using
typography in a distinctive way, but now
extended to cover all forms of visual
devices designed to represent a particular
product or company. The term 'logotype'
originally indicated the piece of metal used
to print an entire word.

Obviously the name and script form of
Coca-Cola is a world-famous logo and
well-protected registered trademark.
However, the very first trademark
registered in the UK was the red triangle
symbol for Bass beer in January 1876.

Bottles of this beer can be seen in
Édouard Manet's painting *A Bar at
the Folies-Bergère* from 1882. An early
example of product placement perhaps?

The art and craft of copywriting △ Generating creative ideas

Right:
Verdi's extravagant opera,
Aida, set in ancient Egypt,
gives us a memorable acronym
which provides a convenient
shorthand for a checklist
of advertising content.
Is your advert entirely in tune?

Singing all the right notes

When it comes to creating an advert, it
can be useful to check that your text and
visual elements fulfil the four 'AIDA' criteria.
This is an old 'mnemonic acronym' –
a memory aid created by using the initial
letters of a series of words to form another
recognisable word.

In this case the acronym spells out the
name of *Aida*, the lavish opera set in Egypt
by Guiseppe Verdi. There are various ways
in which I've seen AIDA spelt out but this
is my version:

grab **A**ttention
impart **I**nformation
promote **D**esire
prompt **A**ction

Just to elaborate on this summary, the
AIDA theory is that your advert needs
to attract the **Attention** of the customer,
deliver relevant **Information**, persuade the
customer that they **Desire** this product or
service, and finally, provide a call to **Action**
that encourages or enables customers to
purchase your product.

Some versions of this opera formula have
the second letter 'I' as 'Interest' – but that
seems a bit daft when you've already
grabbed the customer's attention and so
gained their interest. Far better to include
a bit of information.

You don't necessarily need to tick all
four boxes, especially if your advert is
just part of a larger awareness campaign,
or if people can gather information
from another source, such as a website.
Similarly, you don't always need to provide
customers with directions as to how and
where they can purchase the product
being advertised.

For example, if you're promoting an energy
drink, you don't have to state the obvious
and tell customers that you can buy this
drink at supermarkets, newsagents and
various fast-food outlets. (Isn't it odd that
so many adverts for books end by saying
'Available at all good bookshops', and
there was I about to look for a copy in the
greengrocers.) So, while you might want
to prompt action, there doesn't have to
be a direct or immediate 'call to action'.

Word-check

Mnemonic and **acronym** – and so
we travel from ancient Egypt to classical
Greece. I don't know who gave the Greeks
the right to name so many of our English
writing techniques. Still, if you want to
impress/bore your friends by learning
a few expressions, do feel free to browse
through a book of literary terms.

There are plenty of bizarre classical names
for the clever ways in which we can all
use the English language: *Litotes*, *Meiosis*
and *Zeugma* – to name just the three
Athenian midfield players.

And in case you crave some definitions:
Litotes: ironic understatement.
Meiosis: another word for *litotes*.
Zeugma: using one word to 'yoke' together
two ideas.

But don't worry; knowing what these
rhetorical devices are called in Greek
is really no advantage when it comes to
writing effective copy. These terms are
just a complex way of describing a literary
effect that's already been produced.

The art and craft of copywriting △ Generating creative ideas

Hierarchy of information

An important consideration when you're setting about writing an advert or indeed any other promotional item is what I like to call the 'hierarchy of information'. The great thing about this phrase is that it's pretty much self-explanatory, but just in case you'd like some elaboration, I will explain.

The point is that you have to decide exactly what information you wish to convey to your reader, and then consider which elements are most important and should therefore be most dominant.

What is the key message that you're looking to put across to your audience? How are you going to make sure that this message comes across strongly in your advert?

Many people consider that the best adverts are built on only one strong idea – although I would argue that there are nearly always a number of secondary messages that are carried by various visual and verbal elements in an ad.

For example, you might want to promote a single-minded proposition in your headline, supported and reinforced by an appropriate visual image. That proposition could be stated in a direct way but there is a marked tendency in advertising to intrigue your reader and make him or her work just that little bit harder to get at your meaning. By doing so, they are becoming more involved in your advert.

By way of example, let's analyse an advert for the gladiatorial role-playing PlayStation computer game, *Shadow of Rome*. The key message here is expressed by the graphic image of bloody weapons and a severed arm hanging on a rack. This visual approach is the result of the creative team focussing on a product detail, namely that within this game of gladiatorial combat you can pick up a severed limb and use it as a weapon! Gruesome, I know, but teenage boys love this kind of gory detail.

This notion of extreme action is supported by the headline carved into the wall in the style of Roman lettering, *In the arena anything goes*. Having whetted your interest and piqued your curiosity the body copy goes on to explain more about this game:

Choose your weapon: swords, axes or severed body parts. Then battle your way through ancient Rome, going head to head with centurions, gladiators, elephants and wild tigers. Take part in classic chariot races and infiltrate regal palaces with deadly stealth attacks. Your mission: to restore justice to the corrupt Roman Empire.

Further messages are conveyed by showing the pack shot so it's easy to spot on the shelves of your local gaming or home entertainment shop. Then there's the '18' certificate to show that, due to its violence, this is meant to be an adult game.

In reviewing this hierarchy of information, you can see that this ad also manages to fulfil all four AIDA criteria in that it grabs Attention, imparts Information, promotes Desire, and prompts Action.

Sharpening your style

Above:
Indulge your violent fantasies
in this charming evocation of
classical Rome. Enter the mighty
coliseum, pick up a snack of
larks' tongues and settle down to
watch a Roman gladiator annoy
a very hungry tiger.

Client: CAPCOM
Agency: FEREF
Creative and Art Director:
Neill Furmston
Copywriter: Amers Sehgal

**People are intrigued by an element
of mystery but any interpretation of
an advert by the customer has to be
a fairly rapid process – and the reader
must feel rewarded for taking the
trouble to decipher your message.**

The art and craft of copywriting △ Generating creative ideas

Creative concepts are essential in advertising, but is it possible to teach someone how to be creative – or maybe just that little bit more imaginative? Well, as a copywriter and sometime lecturer who is looking to encourage creativity in myself and others, I'm keen to promote the idea of reading widely and listening carefully. To stay sharp, writers need to be interested in all forms of writing and be aware of all aspects of culture.

You need to consider writing as a skill that you are continually developing. In the same way that a musician improves his playing by listening to other musicians perform and through dedicated practice, so writers can enhance their skills through wide reading and regular writing. A dull and rather obvious statement and therefore true. But if you find reading dull, well, as I've said before, maybe you're not really cut out for a career in copywriting.

By all means seek inspiration and ideas from the advertising that you see and hear around you or that you find in advertising books and archives, but don't restrict your enquiring mind to advertising alone. Try and absorb as much knowledge as you can about popular and high culture because you never know when an obscure piece of information or an unusual idea is going to prove useful.

Magazine articles, short stories, novels, newspaper columns, comic books, art galleries, graffiti, plays, musicals, opera, TV drama, comedy, soaps and documentaries, radio, movies (old and new), sport: they all add to your knowledge of styles and creative references that you can then adapt or adopt in adept ways in your own advertising work.

⊖ beware pickpockets

Above:
Originality can consist of
borrowing ideas from other
forms of popular culture –
including other people's
adverts, as in this clever take
on the iPod campaign, which
won The Chip Shop award
for 'best use of plagarism'.
Trust us advertising folk,
we'll nick stuff from anywhere –
especially if it creates swift
recognition and amusement
for our audience.

Client: London Underground
Agency: Wing Design
Art Director and Illustrator:
Bill Walsh

**Creativity is often about putting
old ideas together in a new way. It's
about making unusual connections
that surprise, delight and inform.**

Word-check

Soap opera – you might be aware of
this already, so forgive me if I'm acting
like the pub bore, but did you know that
the term 'soap opera' has intimate links
with advertising and the early days of
radio shows in the USA?

Weekday radio dramas in the 1930s were
often sponsored by soap manufacturers,
such as Procter & Gamble, who
hoped to influence housewives to
buy their products.

It has been suggested that the 'opera'
element was an ironic comment on the
quality of the drama, and yet all forms of
opera – whatever their setting – deal with
heightened, emotional storylines, whether
it's *EastEnders* in Albert Square or *Aida*
in ancient Egypt.

Thankfully, advertising copywriters can
benefit from a broad interest in all aspects
of culture in an industry where soap opera
is as relevant as grand opera.

The art and craft of copywriting △ **Generating creative ideas** △ Humour in advertising

Avoiding clichés

Be warned: do try and avoid clichés unless you can put a new spin on them. I was tempted to say 'avoid clichés like the plague' but I was concerned that you might have thought I was being serious.

Some words and phrases don't start out as clichés but, through over-use, become trite and obvious. For example, the word 'passion' has been horribly misused in recent years. The effect is that nearly all the passion has been drained out of the word. If it's used appropriately then fine, for example, to describe flamenco dancing or falling in love, but when passion is endlessly misapplied, well, it becomes insipid and empty.

Once you see a word like passionate cropping up in headlines and straplines such as: *passionate about insurance* or *passionate about property*, you know that the original strength of the word has been weakened beyond resuscitation.

An area of the UK calling itself North-East England has been trying to promote tourism to this vaguely-defined area by claiming it has 'passionate people' and 'passionate places'. What a load of old nonsense. Did their agency discover nothing original, unusual or special to say about this region? Did they have to fall back on such a tired cliché?

A commercial cleaning company claims to have 'passionate people' who are 'passionate about laundry' and proudly displays grinning staff on their lorries and in their promotional material as if they just can't wait to get their hands on your soiled sheets and dirty towels.

Frankly, I'd be worried if their staff were passionate about my grubby laundry. To be fair, the writer of their website takes a far more sensible view of matters and provides a breath of fresh air in what could have been a murky cloud of corporate twaddle:

OK, we admit that laundry isn't the most glamorous industry, but we do provide one of life's essential services. No matter how high-tech the world becomes, we will still wear clothes, sleep on sheets, walk on mats, dry with towels and dine on tablecloths (if we're eating at the right places!) – the world will always need laundry!

So you can't live without us, but do you still have to get so excited about laundry? Well probably not. A sheet is a sheet, a towel is a towel, a boilersuit is still a boilersuit – seen one, seen them all. But a towel is only any use as a towel if it's been properly laundered.

How refreshing, how Heineken. Now isn't that honesty more persuasive than banging on about the passion and enthusiasm of your laundry workers? This is getting the message back on track by asking yourself the same question that your customers will be asking: 'What's in it for me?'. Well, in this case, some freshly-laundered towels that your hotel guests will appreciate.

And you know, that's really good enough. Sometimes the most straightforward solution can be the most effective.

He loves me…he loves me hot
Padded balcony bra | **£16**
Low rise short | **£7**

Don't forget Valentine's Day
February 14th

YOUR M&S

Left:
Clever copywriters can wake up
clichés and breathe new life into
hackneyed expresions. Take
this example of the pretty girl
in her scanties picking at a
rose's petals. The writer of
this Valentine's Day advert for
Marks & Spencer could have
fallen back on the standard
expression 'He loves me…
he loves me not'. Being more
creative, the line is changed to
'He loves me…he loves me hot'.

Client: Marks & Spencer

**If you can't find anything new to say
about your client's product, at least
make it sound interesting by putting
a new spin on it.**

Humour, when it's used well, can add a new dimension to your advertising: use it to engage your audience, and make them feel warm and positive towards both your ad and the product.

I believe it's important not to be dismissive of humorous puns and wordplay in advertising. Effective advertising is often about allowing an audience to make interesting and surprising connections – which is also how much of humour works.

Once you start looking at some of the most successful advertising campaigns you begin to realise just how much copywriters rely on wordplay to make their points in amusing and memorable ways.

However, there are bad puns and good puns: the best puns create a witty double take that stops readers in their tracks and makes them sit up and take notice. These clever wordplays can add depth, interest and style to your advert. Bad puns fall flat and leave your reader either groaning or entirely indifferent.

There are several established copywriters who have written books on copywriting who are highly critical of puns and wordplay. But they then go on to quote and praise examples of ads that use those very techniques. It seems they fail to recognise wordplays in the ads they like, while considering such comic techniques a bit shameful or needlessly obscure.

David Ogilvy in his book *Confessions of an Advertising Man* complained in the following way about puns in headlines: 'Some copywriters write tricky headlines – puns, literary allusions, and other obscurities. This is a sin.'

And this on a page facing his glowing praise of one of his own agency's ads for Dove soap, which showed a girl in a bubble bath chatting on the phone with the headline: *Darling, I'm having the most extraordinary experience … I'm head over heels in DOVE*. (As opposed to LOVE. Get it?)

Not only is that a pun, it's a truly terrible, groan-inducing pun that deserves to be punished. In fact, it's a pun even I would shun.

Right:
Adrian Crane created some witty wordplays for a series of 48 sheet posters promoting his advertising agency, Factor 3. These simple yet powerful ads appeared in succession over several months on a large billboard next to a major roundabout, hence one of Adrian's puns, 'The best agency round about'.

Agency: Factor 3
Copywriter and Creative Director: Adrian Crane
Art Director: David Coleman

Sharpening your style

The best agency
round about

Regent House, Rodney Road, Cheltenham GL50 1HX. 01242 254 242   factor❸
APPLIED CREATIVITY

Multiply the power
of your marketing by
a factor of three

01242 254242   www.factor3.co.uk   factor❸
APPLIED CREATIVITY

Ad fab❸

See why some of Gloucestershire's leading companies work with us. www.factor3.co.uk   factor❸
APPLIED CREATIVITY

Generating creative ideas ▷ Humour in advertising

Wordplay is a legitimate copywriting device

Luke Sullivan in his entertaining book on advertising, *Hey Whipple Squeeze This*, takes a massive swipe at wordplay and punning in particular and yet continues to cite great ads that use, you've guessed it, wordplays and puns.

So, he tells would-be copywriters in a bold heading to 'Get puns out of your system right away' and goes on to say:

Puns, in addition to be[ing] *the lowest thing on the joke food chain, have no persuasive value. It's okay to think them. It's okay to write them down. Just make sure you toss them.*

Well, thank goodness – and even occasional greatness – that many of the copywriters he goes on to quote weren't persuaded to be 'tossers'. For if they had tossed away their puns, they would have thrown away some great advertising.

Wordplay is only one tool in the writer's toolkit but we need it like the zoo keeper needs his monkey wrench; I mean the bricklayer needs his trowel. If the technique works, use it.

Right:
This poster campaign promoting The Big Sleep Hotel featured strong typography and witty wordplays with a consistently powerful brand image which gave these ads great impact. It doesn't matter if you fail to pick up on the reference to the novel and film, *The Big Sleep*, although if you do make the connection, it's likely to make you smile and feel slightly clever! Meanwhile the cute letter 'e' on its back offers a nice typographical take on sleep.

Client: The Big Sleep Hotel
Created by Impact Design & Marketing of Taunton in consultation with Lulu Anderson

For example, Luke shows an ad for a travel company aimed at young couples and featuring a variety of exotic landscapes which uses the headline, *After you get married, kiss your wife in places she's never been kissed before*, with its saucy double-entendre on the word 'places'.

Then there's a large poster for Yellow Pages that appears in Luke Sullivan's book with a big cut-out of a cow hiding behind the corner of the billboard plus the word 'Cowhides' and the strapline *If it's out there, it's in here*. This silly pun on a poster is then praised in the caption as being 'One execution from a wonderful campaign…' That's right Luke, it's a pun and it's fun.

Do most advertising pundits have this blind spot where puns are concerned? Can we stop damning writers for being witty and effective? By all means criticise wordplays that don't work or that fail to stimulate interest in a client's products but don't condemn copywriters for using such clever techniques when they often work so well.

Now it's your turn

It's time for another trawl through a pile of advertising. Take up those magazines and newspapers, have a look at all the advertising contained within and pick out where and when the copywriter has used a wordplay such as a double-meaning or a pun.

Make a list of those examples and write a brief review about whether you think the technique is working – or not. Is the wordplay making clever and relevant connections? Is it an obvious pun or does it offer an unusual or original twist that makes you sit up and take notice?

Generating creative ideas △ Humour in advertising

Advertising doesn't have to raise a smile. It can be factual, hard-hitting, surprising, or even shocking. The approach you choose to adopt on behalf of your client simply has to be appropriate – and it has to work.

The pun also rises

Because our language is so flexible and offers such an extensive vocabulary, the English-speaking world is in love with wordplay. Just take a look at the names of hairdressers on the high street with 'The Cut Above', 'Fringe Benefits' and 'Curl Up and Dye'. OK, all very cheesy but then it seems we enjoy this kind of daft word game.

Our newspaper and magazine journalists are similarly obsessed with using wordplay, with a particular fondness for metaphorical and punning headlines. This obsession applies to all types of journal, from the red tops to the posh dailies. If there's a story about railway companies, then you'll have headlines shouting 'Off the rails' or 'Making tracks'.

An issue of the music and culture magazine *The Word* featured an article on young female pop singers in 1960s Paris. The title of this article? *The belles, the belles*. A jokey reference to the hunchback of Notre Dame and Parisian beauty all rolled into one. Well, I liked it! It's silly and apt at the same time. And, blimey, it's even bi-lingual.

The Sun newspaper is especially fond of extreme punning, for example with its jingoistic 'Stick it up your junta' when Argentine troops invaded the Falklands Islands.

Here's another pun from *The Sun* that borrows heavily from Mary Poppins and which won admiration from other journalists, including this glowing tribute from Thomas Sutcliffe writing in *The Independent*:

You don't generally expect to find a literary masterpiece on the back page of The Sun *but if you had looked yesterday you could have seen one… The work in question was a headline – a three-decker which sat above the report of Celtic's shock defeat by a tiny Scottish club, Inverness Caledonian-Thistle. This was an event that called for an exclamation, and some unknown genius had produced a peerless one: 'Super Caley Go Ballistic, Celtic Are Atrocious'.*

It's not difficult to imagine the emotions that accompanied the arrival of the inspiration: the mounting excitement as word after word fell into place, the way in which hardly-daring-to-hope gave way to delirious realisation that every syllable scanned, that the crucial phonemes ('istic' and 'ocious') locked on to appropriate words with the solid clunk of a luxury car door closing.

Domestic violence tears lives apart. For 35 years we've been helping to put them back together.

Left:
A dramatic and emotional image of a family photo literally torn apart in an act of aggression which serves as a powerful visual metaphor for the results of domestic violence. Here the reassembled parts of the photo cleverly indicate the practical support that this charity aims to provide to help put such broken lives back together.

Client: Refuge
Agency: McCann-Erickson

Refuge provides emergency accommodation and support for women and children escaping domestic violence. To support our work make a donation by calling 020 7395 7713, or visit **www.refuge.org.uk**

Refuge

For women and children.
Against domestic violence.

Generating creative ideas △ **Humour in advertising**

CRAVEN "A"

MADE SPECIALLY TO PREVENT SORE THROATS

Ah, the good old days of advertising when you could simply tell bare-faced lies: 'The cigarette that doctors recommend' etc. Alas, those days are gone and in the UK we now have the Advertising Standards Authority (ASA) to keep us in line with their Committee of Advertising Practice (CAP) codes and their goody-two-shoes, Boy Scout motto: 'Honest, decent, truthful and legal'.

It's amazing what you used to be able to get away with. Nobody asked for proof of the wildest claims from manufacturers and advertisers. For example, back in the early days of advertising, right up to the middle of the twentieth century, all sorts of unsubstantiated health claims were made for a wide variety of products including, most notably, cigarettes.

Left:
The first advertising code was drawn up in 1961, and in 1962 the ASA was born. Before then the advertising industry was free to make some outrageous claims as its work went largely unchallenged.

Advertising rules might restrict our creativity unless we're clever enough to work within such constraints and still make memorable adverts that retain their persuasive power.

In the 1940s and 50s a series of ads were run featuring a genial doctor smoking a cigarette with the headline 'More doctors smoke Camels than any other cigarette!'. The exclamation mark takes on new significance from today's perspective of warnings on cigarette packs and our healthy respect for the dangers of smoking.

An even earlier press advert announced that 'Cigares de Joy cure asthma' and went on to claim: 'Joy's cigarettes effect [bring] immediate relief in cases of asthma, wheezing, winter cough and hay fever, and with a little perseverance effect [produce] a permanent cure'. Today, that kind of copy would certainly cause the Advertising Standards Authority to cough and splutter.

Sharpening your style △ **Rules and restrictions** △ Creating effective copy

When it came to outrageous claims, cigarette manufacturers were among the worst offenders but there were many other contenders for the Pinocchio longest-nose award. These ranged from patent medicines that claimed to cure all illnesses to beauty products that would turn back time. (Hang on, don't we still do that? Ah, but supposedly only if there's sufficient scientific evidence to back up your claims otherwise the ASA will swoop down and force you to modify or even scrap your ad.)

Despite what many people think of advertisers and our lack of scruples – our general willingness to sell our own grandmothers, etc – we do now have a set of rules that we must follow. Contrary to popular belief, we're not the constant peddlers of lies that some people make us out to be. In fact, in the honesty stakes, we're slightly above estate agents and only marginally lower than politicians.

Ironically, cigarette manufacturers now welcome those health warnings on packs as being a suitable get-out clause for any future complainants who choose to take up smoking or continue to smoke despite such clear and dire warnings. It was when they failed to warn smokers that manufacturers were left wide open to some very expensive legal claims for compensation due to the serious and often deadly health problems experienced by long-term smokers.

How A Matron Lost 19 Pounds of Fa

Just Dissolved It Away In Her Bath, In One Month.

One minute your bath is filled with ordinary lifeless tap water. Sprinkle in 6 tablespoonfuls of Radox. . . . The next minute that water is super-charged with oxygen gas and impregnated with valuable mineral salts. You step into a bath filled with an artificial mineral water in which you can actually *wash away* your surplus fat. Clever chemists have concentrated in Radox the active ingredients of those European spa waters which are world-famous for their reducing effect. No matter what other course you have adopted, with the additional aid of Radox a more rapid reduction of weight will unfailingly result.

The Matron of a Nursing Home writes :

"A short time ago I took regular nightly Radox Baths for a month, and in that time reduced my weight by 19 lbs. I used a 2/6 packet of Radox each week—7 baths—staying in the bath for 15 minutes at a time. I was 10 stone 8 lbs. before these baths and reduced to 9 stone 3 lbs., and I feel much better in every way. My weight now keeps about the same. I did not diet during the time I lost weight, while taking Radox Baths. I now take three Radox Baths a week, and a 2/6 packet lasts me for 6 or 7 baths. (Incidentally, Radox also removed three troublesome corns and a bunion on joint of big toe, which I had had for years). I recommend Radox to my patients and friends. Please do not publish my name and address, though I should be quite pleased to testify these facts to anyone privately."

4th January, 1932.

The way Radox removes fat is this The oxygen which Radox releases the water opens and penetrates th pores of the skin, while the miner salts act on the fatty deposits, turni them into soluble matter, which dissolved by the water and carrie away into the bath. Deeper-seate fatty deposits move up to the surfa to take their place and are in tu dissolved by further Radox reducir baths, which should be taken at intervals of three days to obtain maximum effect. Step on the scales after a fortnight's treatment with Radox. They will tell the story. **1/6**

NEW GIANT PACKAGES. In t two new GIANT packages : 1s. 6d. a 2s. 6d. (double quantity) at all chemis Radox is more economical than ev

Giant Package

Above:
An early example of highly dubious advertising which suggested that a brand of bath salts could simply melt your fat away! Today, the Advertising Standards Authority still has to be on the lookout for unsubstantiated health and beauty claims.

Below:
Today, some truthful and frightening messages are printed on the cigarette packs themselves. You have been warned!

Keeping a watchful eye on advertisers

The Advertising Standards Authority (ASA) exists – and here I quote the website: 'to make sure all advertising wherever it appears meets the high standards laid down in the advertising codes.' These CAP (Committee of Advertising Practice) codes* go into great detail regarding different product categories and what you can and cannot put in your ads:

The Committee of Advertising Practice (CAP) is the self-regulatory body that creates, revises and enforces the Code. CAP's members include organisations that represent the advertising, sales promotion, direct marketing and media businesses. ... those businesses agree to comply with the Code so that marketing communications are legal, decent, honest and truthful and consumer confidence is maintained.

Anyone has the right to challenge an advert if they think it's offensive or misleading. Just one complaint and the ASA are meant to leap into action and pass judgement.

'Legal, decent, honest and truthful.' Those are the key words that we must honour and obey. As a copywriter, I'm a bit concerned that we have a repetition of honesty and truthfulness, since these words seem synonymous. However, the ASA elaborates on these terms in the following way:

Honesty: marketers should not exploit the credulity, lack of knowledge or inexperience of consumers.

Truthfulness: no marketing communication should mislead, or be likely to mislead, by inaccuracy, ambiguity, exaggeration, omission or otherwise.

And so, as a result of these Codes, are all our advertisements now honest, decent and squeaky clean? Well, those sneaky advertisers do have one or two tricks up their designer sleeves, and sometimes the Codes themselves don't prove quite as effective as they're intended to be, as I'll explain on the following pages.

OK, so we're better
at removing bad ads
than making good ones.

Here at the Advertising Standards Authority, we judge ads on whether they're harmful, misleading, or offensive. Not on whether they're funny, clever or they look good. Which is just as well, really.

Telephone 020 7492 2222 www.asa.org.uk

ASA

Keeping advertising
standards high

Left:
Promoting the work of the Advertising Standards Authority, which keeps a watchful eye on all forms of advertising – and tries to ensure that advertisers do not break the rules.

Footnote
* I've been asked to point out that copyright in the Codes belongs to the Committee of Advertising Practice while copyright in the adjudications belongs to the Advertising Standards Authority. I'm glad we've got that straight, just in case you felt like turning them into song lyrics or something. Now you know you can't without permission.

Telling the truth △ Bending the rules

Are you old enough to drink?

The main principles of the advertising standards codes are that ads should not mislead, cause harm, or offend. There are also specific rules for certain products and marketing methods. These include rules for alcoholic drinks, health and beauty, children, motoring, environmental claims, gambling, direct marketing and prize promotions.

Different guidelines have been developed for broadcast advertising as opposed to non-broadcast advertising and for some reason these tend to be more lenient. For example, press advertising is not meant to show drink in association with heights or swimming and yet TV advertising can. Anyway, here are some of the guidelines for the non-broadcast advertising of alcoholic drinks:

People shown drinking or playing a significant role should neither be nor look under 25 and should not be shown behaving in an adolescent or juvenile way. Younger people may be shown in marketing communications, for example in the context of family celebrations, but should be obviously not drinking.

This is all very praiseworthy but there's a problem with such a grown-up approach to alcohol advertising and that's the fact that *youngsters have always wanted to appear older!* Portraying drinkers who appear to be over 25 suggests a level of sophistication that teenagers will aspire to possess.

Oh well, I suppose it's not easy coming up with a set of rules that will always have the desired effect. However, it would be useful if someone could come up with a way of introducing a more civilised drinking culture in British society that would prevent the spectacle of teenage drunkenness on our high streets every weekend. *Do you wanna have a go, if you think hard enough?* Well, now you can with a creative copywriting exercise.

Left:
Among a number of specialised
categories, specific rules
exist for the advertisement
of alcoholic drinks.

Below:
The fact that this American beer
adopted a recipe which dated
to before the time when drinking
was outlawed in the USA
during the period of Prohibition
enabled me to come up with a
concept which emphasised the
illicit nature of this brew under
the heading 'The beer they
tried to ban'. Well, if it's been
suppressed by the authorities
I'm sure young people will
want to try it.

Client: Concept piece for
Brooklyn Lager
Copywriter: Rob Bowdery

Now it's your turn

Many Mediterranean countries have
cultivated a culture where being drunk
is unseemly, unsexy and unsophisticated.
Can we have an ad campaign which
does that for the UK?

Concepts and copy please for just
such a drink-awareness campaign that
could begin to turn the tide of drunken
behaviour exhibited by too many of
our immature citizens.

Perhaps you'd like to try your hand at
a TV script that promotes the idea that
being in control will result in a much
more enjoyable and successful night out.
Then extend your TV ad into posters
and perhaps even an ambient campaign?
(For more on ambient advertising,
see page 144.)

THE BEER THEY
TRIED TO BAN

THE PRE-PROHIBITION BEER

BROOKLYN
B
LAGER

ON
SALE
NOW

SERVE IT COOL WHEN
THE HEAT IS ON

Appealing to some while offending others

Advertising is not always politically correct or particularly sensitive since it's usually more concerned with getting noticed – and getting its points across quickly. For that reason, advertising can, at times, seem willing to ride roughshod over a group's feelings who aren't necessarily part of their 'target audience'.

Advertisers are always happy to exploit stereotypes for the quick recognition of an idea. For example, adverts aimed at a British audience are likely to make fun of foreign people, not in a nasty way, but by using supposedly comic stereotyping.

And so in UK Adland, Germans will be overweight and keen to grab sun-loungers; the French will be amorous and obsessed with food; Italians will be temperamental yet sexy, etc. In short, it's a handy shorthand. We know our audience will recognise the stereotype and, for the sake of the joke, go along with it.

Similarly, there's a tendency to caricature different types of people in society, so that scientists will be white-coated, bespectacled male boffins with unruly hair while female nurses and secretaries are still likely to be portrayed as sexy or provocative in a saucy seaside-postcard kind of way, or in the old-fashioned movie style: 'Take off your glasses and let down your hair. Why, Miss Jones, you're beautiful'.

This sexual stereotyping can also be reversed for comic effect or to appeal to a more modern female 'ladette' hence the fact that, while it might be considered sexist or even threatening to have a group of lads ogling a young woman in an advert, the reverse situation now seems to be perfectly acceptable with office-working women rolling their eyes while gawping at the Diet Coke man's physique with his perfectly-formed can.

In many ads designed to appeal to women, men will be shown as being obsessed with sport, booze and scantily-clad women. These caricatured men are portrayed as emotionally stunted, largely incompetent, untidy, and invariably unable to cook.

Meanwhile, the women in the ad will be capable of multi-tasking: caring, cooking, cleaning and child rearing with consummate competence while pursuing a full-time career. All very flattering and designed to make women feel good about themselves – and suitably superior to men.

Well, we've got to appeal to our target audience and if that audience is women then, if need be, we're happy to ridicule men, even if we're men ourselves. It's a dirty job and we might be asked to be the enemy of our own sex, but hey, what can we do? It pays the bills.

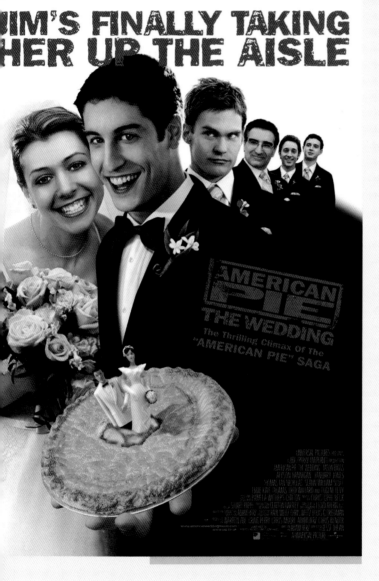

JIM'S FINALLY TAKING HER UP THE AISLE

Left:
It had to be something suitably crude for this American teen movie's third offering. Any movie series that has a naive bloke simulating sex with an apple pie and the cute girl from Buffy the Vampire Slayer describing what she does with a flute is crying out for a vulgar double entendre. Still, you could always argue that any vulgarity is in our dirty minds – so does anyone have the right to be offended?

Client: United International Pictures UK
Agency: FEREF
Copywriter: Chris Kinsella
Creative and Art Director: Neill Furmston

Advertisers can usually get away with overt and old-fashioned sexism by suggesting they're being ironic or 'empowering' people to express their sexuality.

So what happens if an agency produces an offensive or dishonest advert? Well, I'm glad you asked that question. The ASA do have certain powers to force naughty advertisers to mend their ways as the CAP code makes clear:

The vast majority of advertisers, promoters and direct marketers comply with the Code. Those that do not may be subject to sanctions. Adverse publicity may result from the rulings published by the ASA … The media, contractors and service providers may withhold their services or deny access to space.

Trading privileges (including direct mail discounts) and recognition may be revoked, withdrawn or temporarily withheld. Pre-vetting may be imposed and, in some cases, non-complying parties can be referred to the Office of Fair Trading for action.

Advertisers, you have been warned. It's time to get your house in order. You wouldn't want to stir up any bad publicity or court controversy? Or would you? Who was it said, there's no such thing as bad publicity? I know that Oscar Wilde said: 'There is only one thing in the world worse than being talked about, and that is not being talked about'. And it seems the same principle applies to some unprincipled advertisers.

Just because you sell a lot of products to people who should know better doesn't mean you've achieved great advertising. It might mean you have low moral standards.

It's cynical and quite shameless but at times advertisers are happy to offend some people in a bid to appeal to their target audience. French Connection has been associated with a series of contentious campaigns that previously featured their anagram logo: FCUK. Gosh, that looks like the word FUCK. I think I'll have to buy one of their T-shirts to show what a rebel I am. Or, maybe it's time I grew up?

Similarly, Benetton's notorious poster and press campaigns eventually ran out of steam when an increasing number of people realised what a cynical approach it was to feature controversial issues in their ads. After all, their main motivation was to draw attention to themselves and flog a lot of colourful sweaters. They crossed a line when they featured photos of murderers on death row in America and the families of the victims were just a little upset.

More recently, Dolce & Gabbana caused a stir with a series of ads that appeared to glamorise knife crime using stylised tableaux of elegantly-dressed models wielding knives and exhibiting knife wounds. It didn't help that one of the press ads appeared next to a report on a knife attack. But do D&G care about such complaints and the negative publicity they've stirred up? I don't think so. What they're getting is a much bigger splash of publicity thanks to all the press coverage and commentary.

www.ybs.co.uk

Left and below:
A cheeky and eye-catching
concept to encourage students
to think about alternative ways
to pay for their higher education.
Images of a pole-dancer and a
burglar are shown with a sticker
stating 'There is a better way to
put yourself through Uni'. With
student debt on the increase,
there's sure to be a great deal of
interest in any suitable methods
of raising student funds for
life's essentials, like text books –
or do I mean beer?

Client: Concept piece
Art Director: Lawrence Mann
Copywriter: Andrew Newbound
Photographer: Murrindie Frew
www.onemannbrand.co.uk

I'm too sexy for my billboard

One of the hardest tasks facing the ASA is how to judge those ideas and images that should be rejected as offensive when moral standards and viewer expectations are constantly changing. What was considered sexually demeaning in the 1970s can, in the 21st century, be praised for its empowerment of women, or defended as an amusing 'postmodern' ironic statement.

For example, the Playboy bunny logo, which was previously seen by feminists as a crude symbol of male chauvinism, is now proudly worn by many young girls as some kind of cute comment on their own attractiveness and sexual allure. But then again, images of Che Guevara, the communist hero of the Cuban revolution in 1959, have also reappeared on T-shirts, although maybe it's just the funky retro image of some bloke in a beret that appeals to today's teenagers.

Another difficult area for the ASA to police is the supposed glamorisation of violence – and even sexual violence – in certain adverts, especially in the face of advertisers who seek to create highly stylized, 'edgy' images that one can't help feeling have been designed to stir up controversy.

A TV and cinema ad for French Connection showed a particularly violent martial arts fight between two attractive young women that was shocking in its realism. This ad ended with one of the most inappropriate links between sex and violence I've ever seen, where the girls, having beaten each other up, share a passionate kiss which is then cut short by one of the girls headbutting the other.

And this at a time when some youngsters were launching attacks on strangers and using their mobile phone cameras to film their actions, a process euphemistically termed 'happy slapping'. The ASA turned down complaints about this advert while most of the subsequent press commentary concentrated on the fact that the ad featured two girls sharing a kiss. It's a sad reflection on UK society that the British seem to get more upset by sex than violence.

HELLO BOYS.

THE ONE AND ONLY
wonderbra

THE ORIGINAL PUSH-UP PLUNGE BRA. AVAILABLE IN SIZES 32-38 ABC.

Above:
An extraordinarily effective poster campaign for the Wonderbra back in 1994, which managed to appeal to both sexes with Eva Herzigova's well-supported assets displayed to full advantage on giant posters. Many women felt empowered and many men felt aroused. A remarkable shift in moral values since the 1970s when such an ad would have been considered by many people as offensive and even indecent. The *Hello Boys* headline seems to be directed both at the men who will be looking at this cleavage and as a playful reference to the model's own pushed-up boobies.

Client: Wonderbra
Agency: Beattie McGuiness Bungay

Word-check

Postmodern – I really dislike this word in most places where it turns up since its only useful purpose is to describe a stage in architecture when decoration began to be added to rigid and formal 'modernist' structures in the 1950s.

And yet, this pretentious term is bandied about by some media theorists to describe any form of self-aware or ironic communication, as if such self-referencing is an entirely recent occurrence in our overly sophisticated and world-weary culture.

The truth is that advertising – like most forms of entertainment – has always been self-aware and cynical. We are experts at parody, pastiche and all forms of irony. *You don't have to call it postmodernism just to give it some sort of spurious academic credibility!*

Telling the truth △ **Bending the rules** △ Jargon and gibberish

Shock tactics

Somehow it seems much more appropriate to use shock tactics if your 'product' is a worthy one and the message you're conveying is directly relevant. These highly effective adverts for Barnardo's – which were subsequently banned by the ASA despite initial acceptance during early consultation – are for a charity that deals in difficult issues such as child poverty and which wants to create maximum impact on a limited budget by using dramatic headlines and images.

The 'silver spoon' advertising campaign, featured different images of babies in surreal situations – one with a bottle of methylated spirits instead of a milk bottle; another with a cockroach in its mouth and yet another with a syringe. The idea was that not all children are 'born with a silver spoon in their mouth', as the saying goes when someone is born into a well-off family. Instead, in these metaphorical examples, the babies are shown as having something quite different in their mouths.

The overall message was to suggest that childhood poverty and deprivation are not only harmful to young children but that their situation leads to further problems in later life. The charity certainly intended these images to shock but then Barnardo's felt that the situations they represented – children being born into poverty and deprivation – were themselves shocking. As such, Barnardo's wanted a hard-hitting campaign that would raise awareness and get people to react.

Right:
These are indeed shocking images and some people found the advertising so offensive that the ASA decided to uphold their complaints. And yet Barnardo's argues that these are legitimate tactics 'in the fight to support the most vulnerable children in our society'.

Client: Barnardo's

'We believe the images were justified'

Barnardo's Director of Communications, Diana Green, defended the charity's right to use such shocking concepts:

We had to find a way of cutting through this apathy and disbelief and demonstrate how being born into poverty stacks the cards of life against you; that it is likely to lead you to be socially excluded, homeless, to have problems with drugs and alcohol and to commit – or be victims – of crime.

We are pleased we have created a debate about child poverty. People are now more aware that child poverty exists in the UK and are aware it is the biggest threat to childhood. We are pleased we have received many calls to our offices in support of the campaign. We are pleased visits to our website more than doubled in the period of the campaign. We are pleased the numbers of donations received through our website are six times higher than usual.

Rules and restrictions

IF ONLY
EVERY CHILD
IN THE UK WAS
BORN WITH A
SILVER
SPOON

If only poverty didn't crush the
spirit and hope and joy of
thousands of children every year.
If only poverty didn't rob them of
the chance of a positive future.
If only there was no such thing
as poverty. Then there would be
no need for Barnardo's to use
shocking images. There would be
no need for us to ask you to call
0800 032 7222. There would be no
need for Barnardo's to exist. If only.
www.barnardos.org.uk

Barnardo's
GIVING CHILDREN BACK THEIR FUTURE

THERE ARE NO
SILVER SPOONS
FOR CHILDREN BORN INTO
POVERTY

Baby Amy is two minutes old.
Poverty has already mapped out her
future. Poverty is waiting to destroy
Amy's hope and joy and is likely to
lead her to a future of alcoholism.
We can't end poverty but we can
provide the practical skills that Amy
and thousands of others in the UK
need to stop it predetermining their
lives. Don't let poverty destroy
a future. Call 0800 032 7222 or
visit www.barnardos.org.uk now.

Barnardo's
GIVING CHILDREN BACK THEIR FUTURE

THERE ARE NO
SILVER SPOONS
FOR CHILDREN BORN INTO
POVERTY

Baby Mary is three minutes old.
Thanks to poverty she faces a
desperate future. Poverty is waiting
to crush Mary's hope and ambition
and is likely to lead her to a
future of drug abuse. We can't end
poverty but we can provide the
practical skills that Mary and
thousands of others in the UK need
to stop it predetermining their
lives. Don't let poverty destroy
a future. Call 0800 032 7222 or
visit www.barnardos.org.uk now.

Barnardo's
GIVING CHILDREN BACK THEIR FUTURE

✳ ✳ ✳

**It's a great deal more relevant and
legitimate to shock your audience
when your advertising is promoting
a good cause, rather than selling
expensive clothing.**

Telling the truth △ **Bending the rules** △ Jargon and gibberish

Many businesses and organisations are guilty of using jargon that is likely to be incomprehensible to anyone outside their narrow worlds, and so we end up with obscure specialist terms, standard words with special meanings, and a host of names and phrases abbreviated to mysterious sets of letters.

The worlds of advertising, typography and print all have their fair share of specialist expressions and abbreviations that must appear as gobbledegook to outsiders, for example: 'bleed' applies to an image that runs off the edge of a page; 'kerning' describes the minute adjustment of spacing between letters; 'saddle-stitching' is equivalent to stapling a brochure; 'dps' is an abbreviation of double-page spread, and the list goes on.

It can be a convenient shorthand to use such expressions but it does become confusing to outsiders. New members of professions or people joining a particular company are bound to be confused when every phrase or title seems to be reduced to a series of letters, or 'acronyms'.

If your audience can't understand what you're saying then you might as well give up and go home. You're not going to gain any sales by confusing people.

So, what hope is there for someone looking at the adverts produced for these organisations if the same jargon has been thoughtlessly applied? Alas, many clients are so close to their own brand of specialised language that they fail to realise how it can be a huge barrier to understanding.

In the course of my work I've learnt that the drinks – or rather 'beverage' – industry calls instant coffee 'soluble coffee' while, in the lighting industry, domestic light bulbs are called 'GLS lamps' – where the acronym GLS stands for 'General Lighting Service'. Meanwhile lamps themselves are rather romantically yet confusingly known by the French word *luminaires*. Naturally, when you're talking to your customers, it helps to use the language that *they* will understand.

The financial services industry has been guilty of several misdemeanours, not least the use of confusing terminology. For example, many financial companies still refer to their application forms as 'proposals' to the obvious bafflement of their customers for whom a 'proposal' suggests an invitation to marriage: a serious commitment that is likely to prove ruinously expensive in the long term. Ah, I see the connection now.

Rules and restrictions

'Pedagogic cognitive learning inputs'

The academic world is as guilty of using obscure language as most other closed societies. There's a terrible tendency to overcomplicate and nowhere is this more evident than in the language of media theorists, many of whom appear to have adopted a bizarre and outmoded mixture of 1960s French linguistics and Marxist dogma and who are happy to bandy around such tongue-twisting and brain-bending phrases as: 'the hermeneutic hegemony of semiotic paradigms'.

Judith Williamson in her 'seminal treatise' *Decoding advertisements* published back in 1978 states that:

Language is the meta-referent system, a structure of denoting signifiers, while other referent systems are structures of connoted meanings.

Frankly, I do not believe such a complex analysis helps students to understand or create effective advertising.

As another example, the university where I teach part-time describes reading lists as 'indicative resources' which is typical of the kind of baffling language that arises when people feel they must try and make something sound significant and complex, or more 'academic'. Perhaps I'm unusual, but when I'm teaching I always aim to communicate simply and clearly.

Word-check

Jargon – those special words or expressions used by a profession or group that other people find difficult to understand. According to that useful tool, the dictionary, the word originates from late Middle English terms meaning 'twittering', 'chattering'.

However, language that might appear to others as gibberish is likely to be perfectly comprehensible within specialist groups. The problem arises when a particular profession with its own peculiar language tries to communicate with people who are not part of their group.

And that's often when the skills of the copywriter are required to interpret a profession's specialised language for outsiders.

Bending the rules △ Jargon and gibberish

Can we make it any plainer?

One organisation that has consistently campaigned on behalf of baffled members of the public to simplify the language of official documents is the Plain English Campaign. This pressure group was founded by Chrissie Maher in 1979 out of exasperation with politicians, officials, lawyers and business leaders who often use complex language in their dealings with the public.

This organisation has certainly had its work cut out if one considers the mass of confusing gobbledegook and ugly clichés that continue to crop up in official publications and promotional literature.

Marketing managers seem particularly keen on this kind of grandiose language, often peppered with expressions that have crossed the Atlantic in motivational textbooks: 'Our holistic infrastructure leverages our asset resource base impacting customers for enhanced synergistic solutions'. That's the kind of vague nonsense which impresses the David Brent-like characters who apparently populate our sales offices.

The Plain English Campaign has some useful advice on its website as well as examples of how confusing language can be simplified. I include a couple here. I love the one dealing with a request to put up posters in a library. How wonderfully liberating to cut through such waffle.

Crystal clarity?

While I have a great deal of respect for what the Plain English Campaign tries to achieve in terms of simplifying official language, I do have reservations about aspects of their work, including their use of design, layout and typography.

Their crystal logo, in its original guise, was an unprofessional line drawing. This is perhaps not the best way to promote your campaign when image is so important in advertising and good design is an effective way to assist clear expression.

A lack of design awareness was also a shortcoming when I used to see the crystal logo on the back of my bank statements, complete with copious notes, all printed in such a light shade of grey that the words were barely legible! It's no good simplifying your language if you then obscure the result with weak design or poor print processes.

Before
High-quality learning environments are a necessary precondition for facilitation and enhancement of the ongoing learning process.

After
Children need good schools if they are to learn properly.

In a short guide to design on their website, the Plain English Campaign claims that serif typefaces are harder to read than sans serif faces. That statement is simply wrong. If anything, serif faces are easier to read, which is why they are used in most books – including novels and dictionaries – although not this one!

Finally, and this is no reflection on the Plain English Campaign's work, but merely an observation about the perceived shortcomings of companies who choose to use such editing and approval services. What does it say about your organisation if you openly declare that you have to bring in consultants to simplify your language? Do you really want to tell your customers that, without this external assistance, you'd be incapable of communicating clearly? (Why not employ a freelance copywriter? I promise I won't tell anyone!)

Word-check

Serif and **sans serif** – French-sounding terms to describe the two basic families of fonts or typefaces. A serif is the twiddly bit that appears at the ends of letters. Sans serif simply means 'without serifs'. Some examples please:

Serif faces

Garamond   Times
(14 point)   (13 point)

Sans Serif faces

Helvetica   Gill
(12 point)   (14 point)

Supposedly the serif element was designed to mimic the look of handwriting with its twirly characteristics. Today there is a terrific choice of typefaces including some forms with very modest serifs.

And remember, the appropriate use of typefaces can help promote a particular tone of voice while also aiding legibility at different 'point' sizes.

Before
Your enquiry about the use of the entrance area at the library for the purpose of displaying posters and leaflets about Welfare and Supplementary Benefit rights, gives rise to the question of the provenance and authoritativeness of the material to be displayed. Posters and leaflets issued by the Central Office of Information, the Department of Health and Social Security and other authoritative bodies are usually displayed in libraries, but items of a disputatious or polemic kind, whilst not necessarily excluded, are considered individually.

After
Thank you for your letter asking for permission to put up posters in the library. Before we can give you an answer we will need to see a copy of the posters to make sure they won't offend anyone.

Bending the rules △ **Jargon and gibberish**

Sealed with a KISS

In a section that deals with jargon I had to go and use yet another acronym, KISS. But at least it stands for something simple: 'Keep It Simple Stupid'. That's not a bad watchword for advertisers, especially copywriters who might be tempted to use difficult or obscure words in their work.

Generally, it's a good idea to employ a simple word rather than a complex one. You want your ads to be readily understood. Therefore the people at the Plain English Campaign are right to try and cut through complicated official announcements and instructions, but I would like to add a word of caution that this 'one size fits all' approach isn't always appropriate.

Rather than merely simplifying your language, copywriters have a duty to adjust their language to suit their audience. We're back to the idea of using different tones of voice to reflect your knowledge of your readers, listeners or viewers. The audiences that you are going to have to address will vary greatly in their level of sophistication and degree of understanding. You must vary your vocabulary accordingly.

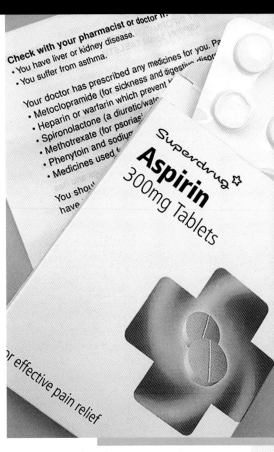

And do remember that a great deal of advertising is not addressed to the public at all but is instead targeted at some highly specialised audiences. Sometimes called trade advertising, this kind of communication is also termed business-to-business – or B2B to use the trendy abbreviation – as opposed to consumer advertising.

For example, a pharmaceutical company might want to send information to general practitioners about a new drug they've developed to treat high blood pressure. You need to use the right kind of language for that specialist audience.

Left:
One of the most important areas where straightforward language is essential is on medical information leaflets: if these instructions aren't clearly understood then the patient could lose more than just their patience.

At such times it's appropriate to employ what would appear to a non-specialist audience as incomprehensible medical jargon, where patients 'present' symptoms, where a condition that increases risk is a 'contraindication' and where blood pressure control is influenced by a group of hormones known as the 'angiotensin-renin-aldosterone system'. Try summarising that little beauty!

I've worked on many B2B campaigns where targeted mailshots, trade press ads and websites have been designed and written to appeal to a variety of specialist audiences. These have included managers of computerised database systems, offshore oil-pipeline engineers, and dedicated medical staff responsible for inserting catheters. Did I use jargon in these communications? Of course I did, or the recipient wouldn't have taken the advertising seriously. You have to speak the language the members of your audience are familiar with since they use it every working day of their lives.

Word-check

TLA – in a stroke of jargon genius, a computer guide to something called 'C++ programming language' features the acronym 'TLA', which stands for 'Three Letter Acronym'. Brilliant, an acronym for acronyms!

And in case you were wondering and perhaps wanted to share this information, C++ is defined as:

a *statically typed, free-form, multi-paradigm, usually compiled language supporting procedural programming, data abstraction, object-oriented programming and generic programming.*

See what I mean about some audiences requiring specialised language?

how to make an innocent smoothie

add loads of this

to lots of these

bin the weird stuff

that's more like it,

magic

innocent. nothing but nothing but fruit

and a nice bit of sunshine

Copy is just one component of an advert and it can play a number of different roles, sometimes supporting striking imagery and at other times taking centre stage.

While this chapter is primarily concerned with the creation of effective copy, I don't want you to lose sight of the importance of visual impact. Whether your advert is enhanced through suitable imagery – photography or illustration – or the use of appropriate colour, layout and typography, the overall impression that any advert makes is dependent on such visual elements.

These various aspects of creative advertising should not be seen in isolation: you need to recognise how they work together to produce powerful communications. A strong idea can be seriously weakened by sloppy copy or awkward artwork.

The best adverts feature elements of design and text that complement one another to produce a persuasive and cohesive unity. In other words, the creative whole is greater than the sum of the various parts. It is the effective collaboration between the visual and the verbal that produces the strongest messages.

The examples that follow show a variety of adverts in a wide range of advertising media. The only ads that don't benefit from an art director's touch or an artworker's skills are radio ads – which is where you have to use other methods to create images in the minds of your audience.

Left:
A fine example of keeping your creative message simple yet striking, which is particularly appropriate for a product which prides itself on its simple, natural qualities. The ads for Innocent Smoothies emphasise the purity of natural ingredients and the absence of any chemical additives – all in a design style which itself has a certain studied innocence and simplicity.

Client: Innocent Smoothies
Agency: Lowe London

Rules and restrictions △ **Creating effective copy** △ Advertising around the world

To make old ideas appear new, you can always employ up-to-date imagery and typography – which is where another element of creativity and originality comes in.

You don't have to be original to be creative. Let me explain that apparent contradiction. I'm not knocking originality in terms of something fresh and new, but there are many ideas – if not most ideas – that aren't original and yet are still effective.

After so many years when advertising creatives have been asked to come up with innovative concepts, it's not surprising that many ideas get repeated or presented again in a slightly different form.

Sometimes we just can't help ourselves. For example, winter is coming to an end and people are beginning to think about trying to get fit again and looking good for the summer. Spring is the season when, depending on your gender (and taste in clothes), people are preparing to bare their flesh in skimpy bikinis or show off their hairy white calves in long shorts.

So, what do the exercise clubs and their advertising agencies do to entice those lardy bodies back into the gym? They produce banners and leaflets shouting *Spring into action*. It happens every year like the return of the daffodils and the flowering of the bluebells. Too corny? Too much of a cliché? Or is this hackneyed headline doing its job quite nicely thank you? Is it perhaps your own creative ego that's insisting on a fresh approach?

What's a hard-pressed copywriter to do? Do we avoid mentioning the season altogether and resist the urge to create a pun out of spring – which is already a metaphorical name for this time of rising sap and natural growth? *Spring in your step*, *Put some spring back in your life*, *Spring into summer*, etc.

Or do we throw down a challenge and make it more personal with some rhyme and alliteration? *Dare to bare!*, *Feeling fit?* or why not offer a comparison: *Will you spend more money servicing your car than maintaining your body this year?* Perhaps we could offer people a discount for annual membership with a wordplay on UK currency? *Shed pounds this week*, etc.

It's not always easy to offer a fresh slant on an old task and sometimes you have to rely on some aspirational imagery of toned bodies to suggest in visual terms that the gym will transform your flabby bottom into buns of steel.

Left:
Motivating people to get fit
isn't always an easy process.
We know people are often full of
good intentions but maybe they
need the services of a personal
trainer to entice them into an
exercise regime. A direct call to
action from The Fitness Team
might just give them the jolt of
energy they require.

Client: The Fitness Team
Agency: Write Angle
Copywriter: Rob Bowdery
Art Director:
Charlotte Kidner Hawkins

the personal approach to your fitness

The fitness team is a Cheltenham-based group of friendly and experienced trainers who are here to help you get more out of life. We offer personal training programmes that are geared to your particular needs.

Whether you simply want to get fit and tone-up or you're actively pursuing a specific sport, the fitness team are your personal coaches who are always on hand to give you practical advice and professional support.

Our training sessions really get results. What's more, your fitness training can be carried out in your home or office, or take place in our own studio. See what a difference a personal trainer makes to your life.

visit our website at www.thefitnessteam.co.uk
e-mail: paul@thefitnessteam.co.uk

for further information call Paul Wanford on 07856 709851

contact us now for your free fitness & lifestyle assessment

Below:
OK, so it might not be
highly original but this phrase
is still wheeled out at the end
of winter – and it's still doing
a reasonable job of reminding
people that they need to get off
the couch and keep off the fries.

spring into **action!**

with a **free** one week fit

Word-check

Original – now there's an interesting example of just how strange, baffling and wonderfully perverse our English language can be.

'Original' can mean something wholly new or, alternatively, an early historic example of such a thing. I suppose everything was original once.

In other words it can be applied to something that is bang up-to-date and brand-spanking new – or, instead, something old from a former era, where it originated.

Ancient or modern – it all depends on how and where you use the word 'original'.

Creativity and originality △ Advertising in unusual places

Right and below:
Suddenly, Dove stole the moral marketing ground from their rivals with campaigns that actually promote, support and celebrate real women of all ages.

Client: Unilever
Agency: Ogilvy and Mather
Reproduced with kind permission of Unilever UK

Dove flies in the face of convention

One of the best examples of copywriting I've come across in recent years is the result of a clever piece of lateral thinking where an old idea has literally been turned around and looked at in a new way. (And yes, I do mean 'literally'; I wasn't using the word for some inappropriate emphasis.)

For centuries, health and beauty products have been promoted as holding back time or taking years off your appearance. Many former claims were wildly inaccurate, but modern statements are subject to medical proof or the Advertising Standards Authority can ask for the ads to be modified or removed.

Advertising often promotes youth and vitality as the main goals in life, which is unfortunate since, as time goes by, it is exactly those qualities that you find diminishing. The only qualities that should improve with age are wisdom and serenity. Well, I live in hope as I head for my second half century.

It seems that a youthful appearance is considered an essential attribute in most advertising and so, while young children strive to look older so they can drink alcopops in pubs, anyone over 30 is meant to be struggling to appear younger. The key message is that we should keep old age at bay. Creams and lotions, pills and diets all promise to keep you looking youthful or even offer to turn the clock back.

Images of svelte, young women fill the pages of our magazines and skip across our TV screens holding out the promise that this or that anti-age product will make you look this young. The truth is, even if we're lucky and don't fall victim to a lethal accident or deadly disease, we all get older, and then we die. Sorry to be so blunt, but there it is. Make the most of the life you have. Oh, and be kind to one another.

Creating effective copy

campaignforrealbeauty.com 🐦 | *Dove.*

lew Dove Firming. As tested on real curves.

As you get older, you begin to resent all this advertising telling you that being old is a bad thing and certainly best avoided – when we know that you can't stop the ageing process indefinitely, unless you want to be cryogenically frozen and spend eternity as an ice lolly.

That's why it was so refreshing that a creative mind came up with the idea of turning 'anti-age' on its head by suggesting that people had the ability and the right to look good at any age. Dove offered skin products that were intended to enhance your looks whatever your age. Dove products aren't marketed as anti-age; they're promoted as 'pro-age'.

It's a brilliant reversal. Dove has recognised an eternal truth and realised that the women they wish to target want to feel good about getting older. Suddenly Dove is on our side, creating products that will enhance our looks no matter how old we are. Rather than rejecting the ageing process, Dove's 'pro-age' campaign celebrates this natural and inevitable progression.

Real beauty lies in the eyes of your consumers

This isn't the first time that Dove has flown in the face of perceived advertising wisdom. While many companies feature skinny models, Dove came up with their 'Campaign for real beauty' which aimed to show that there were many ladies out there who weren't stick-thin size 8 but who still looked and felt sexy and desirable.

It's interesting to note, however, that the shapely ladies featured in the 'campaign for real beauty' ads all have pretty faces while their bodies are curvy and plump rather than irregular and dimpled with cellulite. It seems there's still a fashionable agenda in the representation of bodies that demonstrate 'real beauty'. Oh well, at least we seem to be heading in the right direction in terms of embracing different body forms.

Creativity and originality △ Advertising in unusual places

Creativity can be a contradiction

A clever technique used by advertisers is to take one style of advertising and apply it in an unexpected way to promote something entirely different. We like to play with different media forms and use elements of parody and pastiche to make our ads stand out from the crowd. This contrast in styles may be funny or shocking – but it can certainly make you sit up and take notice.

An excellent example where two very different media forms were made to collide was a piece of direct marketing produced on behalf of Amnesty International by the agency Different Kettle, which combined a charity mail pack with an upmarket fashion catalogue. But I'll let Nick Holmes, the copywriter, tell you all about it. He's good with words:

The brief was to raise funds focussed on the Control Arms Campaign – a campaign run by several NGOs [Non-Government Organisations] including Amnesty. It's a difficult fundraiser as it is a big political issue that needs a big political solution, but it lacks personal stories and a clear tangible use for donors' contributions ie 'Just what can my £20 do to affect such a big issue?'

We decided we wanted to bring the issue of arms (for most of us a distant issue) closer to home. The pack highlights the ease with which arms can be purchased in many parts of the world by using a language (visual and literal) that we are all familiar with – the mail order catalogue.

We originally wanted to call the catalogue Ammo. *When we presented the concepts, Amnesty told us that another agency were developing a TV commercial and that there was a creative overlap. We met the other agency and compared concepts. Their TV shopping brand was called* Teleshop *and so the name was adopted across our work too.*

Although this makes overall strategic sense, it is in my view detrimental to our piece which is a mail order pastiche and nothing directly to do with TV shopping. I would have preferred to stay with Ammo.

Along the way there were some battles over copy – as usual some I won and some I lost. As you can imagine there are an enormous amount of legal sensitivities and this meant I couldn't always be as strident as I would have liked to be. But the secret, as you know, is to keep pushing knowing that you will be pulled back. Start tame and it can only get tamer.

The other issues are those surrounding pastiche: to make it work, you have to be true to it throughout. Clearly the letter is the voice of Amnesty, but the catalogue itself has to be the voice of Teleshop.

This sort of thing can make clients nervous, because they are often tempted to put in a line to effectively say – 'You do realise we're being satirical here, this isn't what we think'. But credit to Amnesty. They held their nerve on this one, and I would like to stress how supportive they were of the whole project.

Creating effective copy

Welcome to Teleshop

where trading in arms is as easy as saying 'load, aim and fire'.

Whatever type of weapon you're after and whatever purpose you want to turn it to, we're confident we'll be able to supply it. Of course there are laws to stop this sort of thing. But frankly they're so riddled with loopholes that any arms broker worth their salt can find a way to sneak through them.

Prices are quoted in pounds sterling, but we'll accept cash in all currencies – we'll even accept diamonds.

So sit back and decide just what carnage and mayhem you want to bring about. Flick through our catalogue to find the weapon that will best do the job. Then place your order. Because whether you're a small time crook, a military dictator, a guerrilla fighter or a drug baron – taking up arms under the current international laws really can be as easy as that.

Please note we are unable to deliver to the UK without the necessary government permits but we're an ideal service for 'friends' and 'families' living abroad. Most other international destinations are catered for. As an experienced arms broker we're used to finding our way round the most bureaucratic obstacles.

Hand guns are all the rage right now. On the streets of Brazil they've claimed over 265,000 lives in the last decade alone. The real beauty of these powerful semi-automatic pistols over the older style revolvers is that they can fire many rounds in rapid succession. This increased firepower is having a real impact out there on the streets.

9mm Pistol
£177.25

Feeling adventurous? Then why stick to guns? The RPG is a shoulder-fired, muzzle-loaded, antitank grenade launcher that can penetrate up to 330mm of standard armour. Just the thing for taking out a light armoured vehicle or attacking villages of unarmed civilians.

Rocket-Propelled Grenade Launcher (RPG) (opposite)
£999.99

Left and below:
When you're dealing with a shocking problem that has devastating results around the world you're entitled to shock and surprise your audience.

Client: Amnesty International
Agency: Different Kettle
Copywriter: Nick Holmes
Art Director: Dave Sturdy

Creativity and originality ▷ Advertising in unusual places

Role reversal

To turn an old idea into an amusing ad, you can always engage in a spot of role reversal. Take the TV ad for the Vauxhall Zafira where this family vehicle is proudly displayed by children who appear to have switched roles with their parents. Their adult conversation succeeds in creating a comic approach that puts across the product features and benefits with wit and style.

Imagine if it had been a straight delivery from adults discussing their purchase and how proud they were of their new vehicle. Hardly anyone would have taken the ad seriously and the whole thing would have fallen flat. Thanks to this clever role-reversal, the serious-minded children generate humour at the expense of their parents who are portrayed as bickering because they're 'over tired' or playing on the beach like excited schoolkids.

Then we have another fine example of role-reversal: or should that be kitchen roll reversal? A straight comparison between two housewives and their choice of kitchen rolls could be toe-curlingly naff. But make those two housewives a couple of stubbly-chinned men in bad drag, looking like a cross-dressing cross between Les Dawson and the female impersonators from Monty Python, and suddenly you've injected new life and humour into an old concept.

You're also tapping into the strange fascination the British seem to have with transvestism. Just what is it in the British psyche that finds such humour in men dressed as women? From pantomime dames to comedy sketch show 'ladies'. This subject could probably form the basis of an entire doctoral thesis for a student of psychology. Whatever the disturbing reasons, the results are usually funny.

Add an intentionally cheesy, 1950s style voice-over for a series of competitive cleaning events between Brenda and Audrey – and you've got a great campaign for Bounty kitchen rolls. The practical advantages are clearly expressed – a highly absorbent paper towel that is also more durable – *and* we've been entertained while that message has been conveyed.

Left and below:
Switching roles can provide a clever twist and inject new life into an old concept. As an added bonus the role reversal process often generates humour to make your ad even more entertaining and memorable.

Left:
Client: Vauxhall
Agency: Lowe London

Below:
Client: Bounty
Agency: Publicis

Word-check

Cheesy – I make no apology for using such colloquial terms as 'cheesy', 'naff' and 'clunky' in my description of adverts since this is very much the kind of expressive language you'll hear when advertising creatives and design consultants discuss their work.

We don't feel the need to use grandiose theoretical terms such as 'semiotic analysis', 'hermeneutics' and 'referent systems'.

In fact, you'll be pleased and possibly surprised to learn that most of the people who work in advertising are refreshingly straightforward in the way they communicate.

Creativity and originality △ Advertising in unusual places

Right and far right:
A contradiction in a headline
can set up an interesting tension
which we hope the reader
will find sufficiently intriguing
to want to discover more.

Right:
Client: Bovis Homes
Copywriter: Rob Bowdery
Art Director:
Charlotte Ward Kidner

Far right:
Client: English Heritage
Copywriter: Rob Bowdery
Art Director: Robin King

A lot of advertising doesn't make sense

Many headlines make use of contradictions: surprising statements that don't appear to make sense until you investigate further to find out their true meaning. The idea is to draw people in with these paradoxical headlines so they read on to gain the explanation.

Of course, this can only work if the headline is sufficiently intriguing but, luckily, it's part of human nature that we want to know the answer to a mystery, no matter how minor. We just can't help ourselves, which is just as well or a lot of body copy would never get read. However, you don't want to make the puzzle too complicated.

Intriguing riddles and wordplays play a major role in advertising and, despite reservations on the part of some critics, they appear to work. In fact they have the merit of involving your audience, actively engaging their interest as they seek to unravel your meaning. So let's take a look at a few press ads and posters which use this technique.

Scandinavian skin

The surprising contrast between cold weather and soft hands provides a good example of how to use contradiction to make a selling point. Neutrogena Hand Cream boldly claims in a press ad: 'In Norway it's always cold. Perfect weather for soft hands.' While most people would consider cold weather to be potentially damaging to their skin with the risk of sore hands, in this ad it is presented as 'perfect weather for soft hands'.

You have to turn to the body copy for the explanation. The text states that Norwegian Formula Neutrogena Hand Cream 'instantly relieves and intensely moisturises even dry, chapped hands'. (Note the effective use of the similar-sounding adverbs: 'instantly' and 'intensely'). The overriding message is that, if this product can work in such tough and testing conditions as a Norwegian winter, then it should certainly perform its function well in less-demanding climates.

Bryn Llongwr, Nell's Point, Barry
2 bedroom apartments from £144,950   0845 000 0000

Get moving with Bovis Homes

prices from
£144,950

Step inside and admire the view

BOVIS
HOMES
www.bovishomes.co.uk

Enjoy a fresh start in a stunning new Bovis Home. Our attractive apartments at
Bryn Llongwyr enjoy a spectacular coastal setting that demands to be seen.
Combined with our fantastic specification and spacious interiors,
these Bovis Homes really do deserve a closer look.

If you enjoy today, get your money back

If you've had a great time on this visit,
we'd like to refund your entry fee when
you sign up today to become a member
of English Heritage.

Join us and you can enjoy free entry at over 400 sites across
the country and support our valuable work of preserving our
magnificent heritage of historic buildings, ancient monuments
and beautiful gardens.

Become a member today.
Speak to one of our staff to find out how.

THREE
MONTHS
FREE

KIDS GO
FREE

ENGLISH HERITAGE
Days out worth
talking about.

Enjoying the view?

A new housing development on a South
Wales headland offered excellent views of
the sea while the interiors of these homes
were also quite attractive. This gave me
the opportunity to create a contradiction
in my headline: 'Step inside and admire the
view'. This line was supported by an image
of a comfortable living room complete
with French windows looking out over
the sunlit bay.

One would usually expect to step *outside*
to admire a view, while there is also an
ambiguity about whether the view referred
to in the headline is an external or internal
one: both views are there to be admired.
Furthermore, the headline can be seen to
provide an open invitation to come along
and view these homes.

Money-back offer

Every year English Heritage attracts
thousands of visitors to its historical sites
around the country. Once on site, a
marketing objective is to encourage
people to take out annual membership.
If you decide to take out membership there
and then you can have your entrance fee
for that day's visit refunded.

This fact enabled me to write an
apparently contradictory headline for
a poster that is displayed at their sites:
'If you enjoy today, get your money back.'
Generally, you would only expect to
get your money back if you'd had a
bad experience. The idea was to intrigue
viewers to read on about the low cost of
membership and the opportunity to reclaim
your entrance money.

Creativity and originality ▷ Advertising in unusual places

Sex still sells

Advertising often plays with our hopes and desires – and preys on our fears and weaknesses. One of those desires or weaknesses is that most of us would like to appeal to the opposite sex (or the same sex if that's your preference) and many adverts will therefore emphasise increased sexual allure and romantic success even if it's only through a vague association with their product.

While the rules on advertising generally won't allow you to make direct claims, it is possible to use various techniques to suggest the powerful aphrodisiac properties of your product. One of the greatest of these persuasive techniques is humour.

Comedy is a sneaky way of suggesting something blatantly but then, if challenged, you can hide behind the ironic humour which allows you to say: 'Ah, but it was only a joke. You're not meant to take it seriously'. Take the successful example of Lynx body sprays aimed straight at the male youth market. Lynx first appeared in the UK in 1985 – following its launch in France in 1983 where the product was and is known as Axe.

The sexy Lynx campaign has been running for years and has achieved massive appeal thanks to its tongue-in-cheek advertising that manages to suggest that, once you spray these products on your body, you'll be irresistible to the ladies.

Beginning with the relatively understated strapline, *The Lynx Effect*, the more recent treatments have featured the somewhat cruder line *Spray more. Get more* while another version has women smelling the Lynx scent and being unable to stop themselves calling out 'Bom chicka wah wah' as some kind of mating call meaning 'Phwoar!'.

The Unilever website makes no apologies for its forthright claims:

With its coolly seductive fragrances and packaging, Lynx deodorant is now the UK's top male grooming brand by coming up with a constant stream of out-there products to give young guys serious pulling power. It must be working because 8 million guys use a Lynx deodorant each day.

Oh well, I suppose it's better than smelling of old armpits and unwashed trainers.

Even before Lynx started making such humorous claims about the amazing sexual pulling power of their products, another brand was doing the same for women: Impulse body sprays, first launched in 1979. In the early TV ads a young woman is seen walking down the street while a passing stranger catches a whiff of her Impulse body spray and rushes off to buy her a bunch of flowers which he then presents to her. The strapline with its neat wordplay was: *Men can't help acting on Impulse.*

Right and below:
A series of promotional cards for Lynx displayed in pubs and clubs to promote the idea that the scent of these body sprays now lasted 24 hours, giving you time to catch up with attractive young ladies right across the world. And how appropriate to use postcards with the various destinations highlighted as being so many hours' travelling time away – with the girls just waiting for you to arrive.

Client: Lynx body spray
Distribution Agency:
Boomerang Media Cards

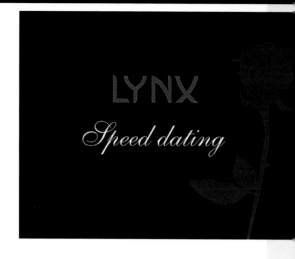

Doing it digitally

One of the more recent media options for advertisers has been the development of digital television where viewers can choose to interact with your advert by pressing the red button on their remote control. It may seem strange that someone would be tempted to switch away from the TV programme they've been watching simply to find out more about an advertised product or service.

And yet for many advertisers this has proved to be a successful way of engaging with their audience. A great number of viewers have actively chosen to interact with adverts and seek further information or entertainment from this digital source. Perhaps it says something about the quality of TV programming – or the slightly unusual habits of digital TV viewers.

Lynx is one of the products that has had fun with this new medium and which has succeeded in entertaining viewers with various interactive options. These have included a form of speed dating video where a girl apparently sits opposite you and you have to decide whether you are going to press a button on your remote control to 'spray' Lynx.

In this particular version, if you don't spray, the prim-looking girl with her hair up and glasses firmly on, remains dull and uninterested. However, if you press the button that 'sprays' Lynx, she lets her hair down, becomes highly animated and starts removing her clothes. Smutty but funny, especially if you're a 17-year-old guy with raging hormones.

Above and left:
Consumers can now interact
with digital advertising and
agencies such as Phosphorus
must therefore develop
entertaining options that
will match or even extend the
brand's identity. Boys need only
press the red button to 'spray'
Lynx and see the amazing effect
this supposedly has on the
opposite sex!

Client: Lynx
Agency: Phosphorus

Word-check

Uninterested – it's useful to make
a distinction between 'uninterested'
and 'disinterested' since the first word is
best used to say that you are not interested
in something.

Meanwhile 'disinterested' has developed
a specialised meaning which is that
you have nothing personal to gain,
or no financial interest in something.

Therefore, if two other people are arguing,
you can be a *disinterested* observer.
You are *interested* in their debate or
argument but you have nothing to gain
from the outcome.

Just to confuse matters, the original
meaning of 'disinterested' apparently was
'uninterested'. This English language stuff;
I didn't say it was going to be easy.

Creativity and originality △ Advertising in unusual places

Sometimes it pays to tell it straight

Just a word of warning: remember that we're in the business of promotion and sales. Advertising can be seen as a form of entertainment, and it's often the most unusual and amusing creative ideas that win advertising awards. However, these awards do not always reflect an advert's actual sales achievements.

Therefore, at times, it might pay to sacrifice your cleverness and style for a very simple and straightforward message. Is it actually any more effective to promote a shoe sale with the word-playing headline 'We're stamping down on prices' rather than using the simple statement '50% off all shoes' or 'Half-price footwear'?

Why over-complicate your message when a simple statement might get your message across more quickly and more powerfully?

But remember, it's not always easy being simple. Another paradox. What I mean is that it can take a great deal of time and effort to pare something down to its essentials; to establish the single message you wish to convey and then present it in a very direct and immediate way.

One classic example of such directness is the long-running campaign from the manufacturer, Ronseal, with their range of varnishes and wood stains. Despite its simplicity, this is a very clever and effective campaign, employing the well-established strapline, *Does exactly what it says on the tin*.

This straightforward approach, voiced by a tough, no-nonsense builder character, is an excellent way to indicate honest and reliable products that will deliver on their promises. Ronseal has gone to the trouble of protecting their intellectual property in this strapline by registering it as a trademark in their business sector.

The simplicity and directness of this phrase has been so widely appreciated that it has now entered the English language not just as a popular catchphrase but almost as a proverbial expression to describe any trustworthy process or reliable product.

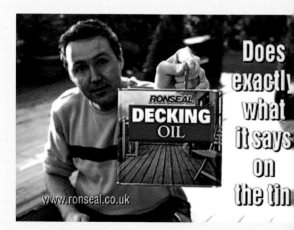

innocent smoothies
nothing but nothing but fruit

Above:
A further example of
straightforward advertising
with a direct message from
Innocent Smoothies to
emphasise this product's
own natural simplicity. So pure,
it bears repetition: *nothing but
nothing but fruit*.

Client: Innocent Smoothies
Agency: Lowe London

Left:
The straightforward,
direct approach of Ronseal's
long-running campaign
has been so successful,
its strapline has now entered
the English language.

Client: Ronseal

**Sometimes clever copy or complex
concepts can be a barrier to clear
communication. Could your message
be simpler?**

Creativity and originality △ Advertising in unusual places

There are so many places where you're likely to find adverts these days. I'm sure there's a researcher who will offer a precise figure for the average number of ads you'll see in a day, although that rather depends on the kind of day you're having. All I know is that there is a huge number of advertising messages out there competing for our attention.

Take a trip to the supermarket and you'll find ads slotted into your shopping trolley. There will be further messages on the shopping bags plus various promotional leaflets and posters at the check-outs. Then as you're wandering round the aisles, you're likely to see 'floor vinyls' beneath your feet and perhaps some 'shelf wobblers' sticking out from the shelves promoting specific products.

It seems that ads are inescapable and advertisers and their media buyers are keen to find new ways to grab your attention and new places to place a promotional message when you're least expecting it. Pubs and clubs even have small poster sites on the backs of their toilet doors. Talk about a captive audience. And what about those ads positioned over urinals? Who says blokes can't multi-task? Now there's something to hold a lad's attention while he's busy holding something else.

This more unusual kind of advertising is often called 'ambient' since it seems to pop up anywhere and appear all around us. There was a great example that featured a plastic splash mat positioned within a urinal which was used to recruit would-be firefighters! Another of these lavatorial ads showed the image of a car which, when you peed on it changed into the image of a smashed-up vehicle to warn you of the dangers of drink-driving.

This is all good stuff which demonstrates lateral creative thinking in action. The Edinburgh-based agency, Family, has the ability to conjure up some excellent ambient advertising. Take a look at these superb examples created on behalf of their client, Scottish Slimmers.

They've taken the idea of targetting people who would like to lose weight and then thought laterally – or perhaps I should say, widely – as to where best to position their ads. And so we have the tight squeeze on the station's narrow entrance gates and the visual pun of the weighted down taxi. Simply brilliant.

Once you start looking at a problem from a different angle you can start generating some unusual responses and spark your imagination into action with innovative concepts and copylines.

Above and left:

Applying lateral thinking to the problem of expanding waistlines has led to some innovative ambient media solutions from this highly imaginative agency.

The Scottish Slimmers taxi had its suspension severely lowered at the back and raised at the front, to give the impression that somebody particularly heavy was in the back of the cab. Meanwhile, the narrow entrance gates at the station provide an excellent place to remind people of their width.

Agency: Family
Client: Scottish Slimmers –
'Tight squeeze'
Copywriter: David Isaac
Art Director: Kevin Bird

Creativity and originality ▷ Advertising in unusual places ▷ Writing to fit

Say knickers to boring ads

Another classic example of ambient advertising was created on behalf of an underwear firm called Bamboo Lingerie whose agency arranged for the following cheeky message to be stencilled on the New York sidewalks outside the venue of a fashion convention: 'From here it looks like you could use some new underwear.'

Not only did buyers and consumers see this message, but thanks to its originality, the press noticed it too and hundreds of articles were written all over the world about Bamboo Lingerie – and so, despite a limited budget, the message spread.

There was some fear that the company would be prosecuted for defacing public property but the stencil-operators had used water-based inks that were easy to wash off. This legal dimension is another factor that ambient advertisers need to consider.

There are rules and regulations governing how and where you can advertise. It's all very well wanting to be a maverick and edgy agency that boldly advertises where no advertiser has gone before, but if you're sticking your ads where they're illegal and unwanted then you can get your agency and your client into big trouble and large financial penalties.

Word-check

Ambient – a trendy area of advertising where ads pop up in surprising places and make use of their surroundings to create even greater impact with an audience who can then interact with the promotional messages in a more immediate way.

Despite the modern media excitement when such 'guerrilla' advertising occurs, this is not a new concept. In his novel, *The Sun Also Rises*, published in 1928 and based largely on his own experiences, Ernest Hemingway recalls how people were employed to walk around the streets of Paris with a water-soaked roller that printed a wet message on the pavement promoting the aperitif, *Cinzano*.

What a great idea! Perhaps it's something about this drink – or its marketing team – since *Cinzano* was also the first product to be advertised using neon lighting, again in Paris, in 1913 – or 1912 – depending on your source.

Right:
McEwan's ale is presented as being so good that the beer mat wants you to spill some so it can have a taste. The Glasgow-based agency Frame came up with this award-winning copy treatment.

Agency: Frame
Client: Scottish Courage/ McEwan's – 'Beer mats'
Copywriter: Adam Smith
Art Director: Phil Sanderson

Creating effective copy

Long copy that simply demands to be read and keeps you entertained and informed as it conveys those all-important marketing messages

Increasingly, advertising seems to be cutting down on copy. We are endlessly told 'less is more' and that 'nobody reads body copy'. In fact, people go on about it at great length. They consider that modern advertising is all about image and our audiences are visually literate but verbally stupid. Well, I don't subscribe to that view since I believe that long copy, if it's well-written, will be read. And while short copy can be great fun to write, long copy is damned hard work.

With long copy, each phrase and every sentence has to be shaped, adjusted and amended since, even if the customer isn't always going to read the brochure from cover to cover, your client certainly will. And to be fair, even if customers are only dipping into the content, everything you say, wherever it appears, must make sense, be easy to read and convey the right impression.

What's more, organising your content is always going to be harder when you're writing long copy rather than putting together a short ad or a brief website banner. Short copy can be written in the pub. You can scribble ideas down on the back of a beer mat and then type them up when you get back to the office. Now, that's my idea of a great job. Whereas long copy can be a time-consuming slog.

USING US BEERMATS TO STOP TABLES WOBBLING?
WHAT DID WE EVER DO TO YOU?
BEERMATS HAVE DREAMS TOO YOU KNOW. WE LIVE FOR
WOBBLY TABLES. THEY GIVE US A SLIVER OF HOPE.

WE LONG FOR THE DAY THAT A HAND WILL PLACE
A PINT OF McEWAN'S ON US. THE TABLE
WILL ROCK, LEFT, THEN RIGHT, THEN LEFT AGAIN.
A DROP OF McEWAN'S WILL ROLL DOWN THE GLASS.
AND FOR ONCE IN OUR PITIFUL LIVES,
WE'LL ACTUALLY GET TO TASTE SOMETHING...

LET THE DREAM LIVE.

LET THE TABLE WOBBLE.

THE REAL

DEAR BEER DRINKERS.

LIFE FOR US BEERMATS IS SLIM – A FEW HOURS,
A COUPLE OF DAYS AT BEST. THEN A QUICK FLIP
AND FOLD FROM A CUTE BARMAID,
AND OFF TO THE BIG RECYCLING BIN IN THE SKY.

ALL WE ASK BEFORE WE POP OFF IS;
LET US TASTE SOMETHING. NEXT TIME YOU'RE
SAVOURING YOUR PINT OF McEWAN'S, AND YOU
SEE A TASTY DRIP ROLLING DOWN THE GLASS,
HOLD YOURSELF BACK FROM LICKING IT.

LET US TASTE THE REAL McEWAN'S.

CHEERS, AND ENJOY.

THE REAL

Right:
The content of this ad for VSO deals with relevant issues for commuters such as careers and work, and suggests that people with skills can make a real difference in impoverished communities while gaining some profound emotional and spiritual rewards.

Client: VSO
Agency: Kitcatt Nohr Alexander Shaw
Copywriter: Paul Kitcatt
Art Director: Maya Rowson

Who has time for long copy?

Short copy certainly has its place and can be swift, immediate and a suitable complement to a strong, image-led ad. But there are places where long copy ads can be very effective – and that's where people have the time and inclination to read them.

Long copy press ads can still work well, especially in the 'quality' newspapers, but they have to be well written. Editorial-style 'advertorials' are also a cunning way of promoting products in the guise of a magazine or newspaper article, and they inevitably call for long copy in a suitably journalistic style.

But the ideal place for long copy ads is where your audience has plenty of time on their hands and nothing much else to do with it – apart from reading your ad. Public transport provides just such opportunities.

London Underground station platforms with their giant curved ad spaces and the inside of tube trains where the ads appear above your head – these are places where you have a captive audience, either waiting for their train or sitting in it, studiously avoiding eye contact with their fellow passengers. (Well, we are British after all.)

Take a look at this long copy ad for the VSO, or Voluntary Service Overseas, a charity which relies on people taking a couple of years out from their careers to give something back, working in a disadvantaged community somewhere in the so-called Third World.

Such ads have been written with their location and purpose very much in mind. They will be read by commuters as they wait for their train or sit in a carriage and so they have time to take in some longer copy.

If your message is strong and your copy well-written then, as long as the ad is well-positioned, there's no reason why it shouldn't also be well-read.

Creating effective copy

Will you remember today forever? You went to work. The tube was strangely empty. You got a hilarious email. Someone made you a perfect cup of tea. You ate a delicious sandwich. The photocopier did not jam. There were no delays on the tube home. But will you remember today forever? You saw an ad on the tube that changed your life. You decided to do something about the state of the world. You offered your professional experience to VSO. You volunteered to share your skills in the world's poorest communities. You stood up not because there were no seats, but to be counted. To say you wanted to make a difference. This is your chance. This is the ad. This is the website: www.vso.org.uk. This is the number: 020 8780 7500. This is the day.

VSO
Sharing skills
Changing lives
Registered Charity Number 313757

Instead of standing waiting for a tube train, you're swimming lear waters. And suddenly, in front of you, this is the shape that A bottlenose dolphin, hugely intelligent, powerful, playful actly this size. • These are the creatures we are privileged to e planet with. We can respect them, or we can destroy **them.** an see bottlenose dolphins around the shores **of the UK.** nore, you can adopt one yourself, or as a **gift for someone** ese magnificent warm-blooded cr**eatures can often be** ng on the bow waves of ships **at sea. They love to play at** out they don't need board**s, and they don't 'wipe out').** • Dolphins y can leap ten feet or m**ore out of the water. •** Dolphins ying games with **all sorts of** things, and other animals, e they like playing **with, of** similar intelligence, is called homo They are **social, tend**ing to live in families or groups called **of anything from** two or three dolphins to 500. They spend **f time with clo**se family members or friends – females the fa**mily's young** calves. But males tend to form their own (If there we**re do**lphin bars, the males would stand at them.) es make friends with other families, and support each other of hardship. Dolphins work out clever ways of catching food, ng on where they live. In some places they chase fish onto

the shore, then roll up on the beach to catch them. And bottlenoses **have** been seen "fish-whacking" – stunning fish by flicking them in **the air w**ith their tail flukes and then picking them off the surface **of the water.** • **The** bottlenose dolphin is just one species of **whale. Large and small, th**ere are more than 80 species of **whale in the world's oceans. And** large means just that. A blue **whale's arteries are as big as drain** pipes, and its heart is **the size of a small car. Its tongue weigh**s 4 tons, and is so **huge that a football team could stand on** it. • Whales **are still hunted and killed deliberately by a** land-living **mammal only 6 feet high. And even greater nu**mbers are accidentally killed **by human activity – through being** caught in nets, or choked by the fil**th ships throw overboard. •** We fight back, on their behal**f – and b**y supporting **WDCS, y**ou can help us fight to make the **seas** cleaner and put an end **to w**haling for good. And if you'**d also** like to extend the flipper of frie**nd**ship by adopting a dolphin, you can do that through us as well. Just go to our website: www.adoptadolphin.com, or phone us.

It's not often we can show you what you'll get, life size, when you adopt a dolphin. Thank you, Viacom, for giving us this poster site so we could.

— LIFE SIZE ————————————————▶

Join us
extend the flipper
of friendship

Whale and Dolphin Conservation Society
Tel: 0870 870 5001   www.adoptadolphin.com
Registered charity number 1014705

WDCS

Above:
This long-copy ad for the Whale and Dolphin Conservation Society was a successful competition entry which makes clever use of emboldened letters and words picked out of the detailed message to show the silhouette of a full-size dolphin on a London Underground poster site.

Client: WDCS, the Whale and Dolphin Conservation Society
Photographer: Mark Carwardine

Creativity and originality △ Advertising in unusual places △ Writing to fit

'The advert now waiting at Platform 2'

The London transport system offers a great number of advertising opportunities and a large audience of commuters, travellers and tourists. In marketing terms, there are a great number of 'opportunities to view' so it can be highly cost-effective to run ads that reach out to so many people.

What's more, these people often have time to take in some detailed messages. Among the many sites that can be exploited by advertisers are the wall posters above the escalators which convey people at a fixed speed, right next to your adverts.

This steady progression lends itself to some novel treatments, where you can establish a theme or build up suspense before hitting your audience with the reveal. Alternatively, you can simply bludgeon your audience over the head with repetition. (The musical *Chicago* simply blitzed the walls with a series of sexy images of their dancers from the hit show.)

On this spread you can see a fine example of a build-up campaign with a series of mini-posters that would certainly engage your intention and intrigue with what appears to be an accumulation of insults:

You stink; your teeth are stained black; your breath smells of onions and cheap rum; you've worn the same jacket for the last six months; you've got venereal disease [etc].

Are they talking about your fellow office workers travelling on the Tube? It's only when we near the end of the escalator that we discover the ads are referring to the typical soldier in the British army of 1808 and that you can learn more about the life of such soldiers at the National Army Museum.

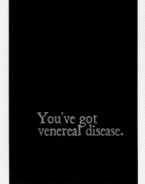

Your breath
smells of onions
and cheap rum.

You're the
pride of the
British Army
in 1808

You've worn
the same jacket
for the last six
months.

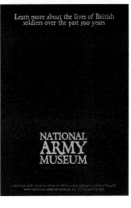

Learn more about the lives of British
soldiers over the past 500 years

NATIONAL
ARMY
MUSEUM

Now it's your turn

Pick one of these three organisations
and create a long-copy billboard advert
to appear in London Underground stations.
Your ad must raise awareness of the
activities of the particular charity or
pressure group. You can use imagery
but it should be kept to a minimum.

Fairtrade
Amnesty International
Friends of the Earth

All these organisations are quite complex
and so you'll need to research their
activities in some depth to get a good idea
of their aims and activities. Only then
can you decide exactly what information
you wish to convey.

Do you want people to think with their
heads or their hearts? And which approach
is likely to deliver the greatest response?

Above and left:
One of the most attractive
features of this intriguing series
of statements running next
to the London Underground
escalators is the simplicity
and strength of the concept
which manages to achieve
impact through clever copy
and effective typography
using 'aged' lettering and
richly textured colours.

Client: Concept piece for
National Army Museum
Agency: Golley Slater
Copywriter: Philip Hickes
Art Director: Dave Abbott

Creativity and originality ▷ Advertising in unusual places ▷ Writing to fit

Keeping it direct

Another area of advertising where long copy is often appropriate and can produce excellent results is direct mail. This form of direct marketing, where the copywriter usually knows a fair amount about the person receiving the mail pack, allows you to create much more immediate messages and encourages you to enter into a more personal correspondence.

Whether it's a charity mailing outlining the progress that's been made to provide clean water to families in Africa or a catalogue describing some exotic new destinations for adventure holidays, you'll know that your readers are likely to want to read on and find out more.

Here are some examples of effective direct marketing for Saga holidays and Voluntary Service Overseas (VSO). As you can see, while Saga is keen to tempt the over 50s into exotic holidaymaking, not all advertising is trying to sell you something. The VSO mailing cards are actually inviting you to give something back. And perhaps unusually for a charity, they're not after your money but rather your time and your skills.

Direct marketing gives you the opportunity to engage your reader with more detail, which you can impart at greater length. For example, within your mail pack you can include case studies, personal endorsements, celebrity interviews or whatever else will interest and add credibility to your message.

Right:
Saga is a highly successful brand with more than 20 million customers, all of whom are over 50. Their biggest marketing challenge is trying to appeal to the 'new' over 50s since people who have just passed this milestone are often in denial of the fact! The copy content of this mail pack aimed to dispel the myth that Saga were just about coach tours for the elderly. With over 60 countries on offer, it was time for people to 'think again' about Saga holidays.

Client: Saga Holidays
Agency: Target Direct

Creating effective copy

SAGA
Think again

If you think Saga's holidays are just about coach tours, think again – we can take you to hundreds of exciting destinations in over 60 countries worldwide, and offer safaris, cruises, all-inclusive holidays and more.

With a Saga holiday there are no regrets. In fact, last year, of the 86% of our travellers who completed their holiday questionnaire, 97% rated their holiday as either excellent or good. With over 50 years' experience, our Price Promise and thousands of holidays with no single room supplement, it really is time to think again about Saga.

Choose from our diverse range of brochures
● Europe and the Mediterranean
● Travellers World *(Worldwide holidays)*
● Saga Rose and Saga Ruby
  (Saga's own cruise ships)
● River Cruising
● British Isles and Ireland
● Christmas holidays 2004
● UK short breaks
● European short breaks
● Holidays exclusively for singles
● Music Review
● Gardens Calendar
● Verona Opera Festival

"If we have one regret, it's not sending for the brochures sooner."

Order your brochures today
Call FREE on **0800 056 5079** quoting reference MAG2
or visit www.sagaholidays.co.uk

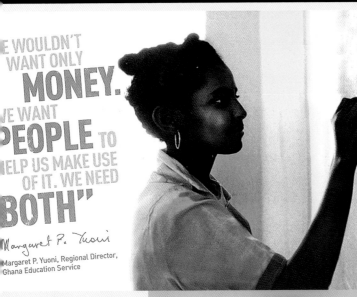

E WOULDN'T WANT ONLY **MONEY.** E WANT **PEOPLE** TO HELP US MAKE USE OF IT. WE NEED **BOTH"**

Margaret P. Yuoni
Margaret P. Yuoni, Regional Director,
Ghana Education Service

VOLUNTEERS USE THE SLEEPING **POTENTIAL** **PEOPLE** HAVE. THEY HELP PEOPLE TO **HELP** **THEMSELVES"**

Alasidongor B. B. Emmanuel
Alasidongor B. B. Emmanuel,
Teacher, Ghana

Left:
For these Voluntary Service Overseas (VSO) postcard mailers, the headline copy was taken directly from written statements made by local workers in the countries where volunteers were most needed. This gave the headlines great strength and immediacy, creating a personal appeal from the people on the ground who were happy to add their signatures to these direct requests for assistance.

Client: VSO
Agency: Kitcatt Nohr Alexander Shaw
Copywriter: Paul Kitcatt
Art Director: Maya Rowson

Remember, direct mail is only junk mail if it hasn't been targeted to the right audience. If your message is directly relevant, then there's every chance that it will be read.

Creativity and originality △ Advertising in unusual places △ Writing to fit

One of the greatest skills you need to develop as a copywriter is the ability to edit your own work. If you can cut out surplus words that don't add sense or style to your copy – then be ruthless.

Ideally, you need to distance yourself from your own work and look at it through fresh eyes. Be cold and clinical in your assessment. You need to be your own harshest critic who won't be happy with your text until it's been pruned, polished and perfected.

You don't have to be self-critical in a negative or destructive way but in a wholly positive way. It's all about positive self-doubt, reviewing your text objectively with a view to making improvements. Can it be made any better? Is your meaning clear? Is your text sufficiently entertaining and persuasive? Could I have said all that in fewer words?

Try and view your own ideas and copy as if you're seeing them for the first time. Can they be improved upon? Usually they can. That's why your editing process is so important.

Right:
A fabulous use of bubble wrap to enclose this card which invites recipients to voice their opinions, lodge a complaint, or in other words, 'have a pop' at railway services. Neat, short copy, a clever wordplay and all due credit to the team who developed this creative concept.

Client: Rail Passengers Council
Agency: Kitcatt Nohr
Alexander Shaw
Copywriter: Simon Robinson
Art Director: Maya Rowson

**Top tips for text –
or how to make your copy seductive, irresistible and oh-so-sexy**

I couldn't resist having a go at a hard-sell headline. I do want to give you some practical tips but I can't guarantee instant seduction each and every time.

One of the most useful suggestions I can give you is to keep your copy short, sharp and punchy.

Yes, you want to inject the appropriate character and style into your writing to suit your audience, but do try and keep it simple and direct. Even a sophisticated audience would generally prefer to get your message quickly and easily. People with busy working lives don't want to waste their time.

You need to discipline yourself to use short headlines, short sentences and short paragraphs. It's so much easier to understand words if there aren't too many of them – and when they're not too crowded together.

Creating effective copy

DON'T JUST HAVE A POP

MAKE YOUR VOICE HEARD

If you run your words together to produce one big block of undivided text then the reader's eye is likely to skate all over it and be unable to find any purchase or point of entry.

Use appropriate paragraph breaks. In fact use paragraph breaks even if they aren't required grammatically but simply to make your text easier to view and digest.

Some designers have an unfortunate habit of not reading your words and then removing your carefully chosen paragraph breaks to create a deathly tombstone of text. I think they assume that no one else is going to read your copy so why not tidy it all up and cram it into a neat block since that will be easier to place in their design. (Designers, if you're still reading this, please take note!)

Another useful tip if you do need to write long copy is to break up any lengthy stretches of text with suitable subheadings. That way your reader can have a bit of a breather and catch up on the key messages in the various paragraphs simply by scanning your headings.

Once again, this is where the notion of the 'hierarchy of information' comes into play. You must try and shape your content to fit a natural order, with one idea flowing seamlessly into the next, building up a logical and persuasive argument as to why this particular surgical truss is the most suitable for hernia-sufferers, or whatever the product is you're trying to flog.

Advertising in unusual places △ **Writing to fit**

Sound reasons for using radio

Although sometimes seen as a poor relation of TV advertising, radio advertising has a great deal to recommend it. Radio recordings needn't be expensive to produce and, thanks to the many ways in which you can now listen to commercial digital radio, there are more opportunities for your listeners to hear your ad. Funnily enough, the example of radio advertising included here was used to promote digital radio advertising.

And you know what I really like about radio advertising? *The importance of the words*. Words take on a new significance because they have to work so hard. On radio you only have your audience's ears to play with which means you must make the most of your script, sound effects (or SFX to use its funky abbreviation) and, if required, music.

I want to show you an example of a radio advert script produced by some of my students who might have won recognition at the D&AD Student Awards if the fools had got round to submitting it. The moral of this story is, don't sit on your best work when you need to show the world what you can do.

One of the greatest advantages of radio is how you can use words and sounds to suggest the most surreal scenarios or complex situations. To translate these mental pictures for television or cinema would not only cost a fortune but could also diminish their comic impact.

For example, in the following radio ad it's a great deal funnier to try and *imagine* DAB radios as great galumphing animals looking for a digital mate rather than literally picturing them on screen. And then there's the fun you can have creating oddly appropriate sound effects to match these weird creatures.

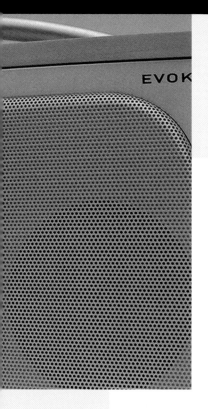

Left:
Radio is an unusual and liberating medium for copywriters since, to see what's being said, the words and sounds you select have to conjure up suitable images in the minds of your listeners.

Below:
The Digital Plain
Creative Team: Paul Robbins, Andrew Singleton, Samuel Turk
Advertising students at the University of Gloucestershire

The Digital Plain

[The script is voiced by a David Attenborough soundalike]

[SFX – weird mix of digitised animal cries/noises and radio transmission sounds.]

Welcome to the world of digital radio advertising. Here on the digital plain, an extraordinary variety of radio life forms live and flourish. Listen carefully and the distinctive mating call of the DAB radio can be heard.

[SFX – DAB radio mating calls.]

Competition for attention is fierce. Here a pair of home computers compete for online dominance. At full volume their communication can be exceptionally far-reaching.

[SFX – PC cries echoing across plain.]

Meanwhile, a herd of iPods is searching for fulfilling relationships. Indeed, the successful downloading of podcasts often results in lifetime commitment.

[SFX – Romantic music, plus noise of iPods climaxing with all sounds increasing in volume]

[Commentator has to raise his voice to be heard over crescendo of sounds]

With such an increase in digital media options, now more than ever, the world of radio advertising is alive with possibilities.

To hear more, tune into www.rab.co.uk

Advertising in unusual places △ Writing to fit

Advertising in the digital age

The importance of paring down your words and conveying information quickly is nowhere more important than in the brave new world of digital media.

Websites, online advertising, e-mails, and texting have joined the ranks of established advertising media – and even replaced some traditional forms in the promotional mix. For example, many companies no longer produce expensive printed brochures and newsletters but choose instead to convey that information online.

There's really no need to be afraid of new media forms; you simply need to understand how they work and then adapt your content to fit that format. As in all advertising, I'm pleased to report that content is still king and, once again, it's the most persuasive combination of words and images that's going to prove most effective for websites. Although you also need to be aware of how search engines rank sites and include appropriate key words.

When it comes to writing text for websites, there really is a need for speed. Keep your message simple and direct – and relay your information quickly.

In the past, too many computer geeks have claimed to be 'website designers' when they should more aptly be termed website technicians. Please remember that the roles of graphic designer and copywriter are still of the greatest importance for digital media and their absence is all too apparent when you open up some websites with their poor layout, clunky appearance and woeful text riddled with typographical errors.

Copywriters working in this modern medium must be aware that people searching for information online are nearly always in a hurry. They want instant gratification, clear content, ease of navigation and simple instructions. They don't want to wait a long time for your pages to load and they don't want to wade through reams of text.

Reading on screen is not a very comfortable process. It's liable to lead to eye-strain so we all want websites to make their points quickly. We also want clear navigation that tells us where we can click for further information when we want to explore something in more detail.

That good old 'hierarchy of information' is critical in website design and you must put all the right details on the hard-working home page which often serves as your shop window, entrance door, billboard and table of contents all rolled into one.

Creating effective copy

Boost your online sales
with **SpinMe** photo-rotations

By using **SpinMe** photographic rotations on your website, your customers will be able to view your company's fashion clothing and accessories from all angles – and gain greater confidence to make shopping purchases online.

The result is increased sales – and fewer returns. That's because your customers have every opportunity to judge the all-round look of your fashion items prior to purchase.

And the cost of this service?

You might be suprised to learn that a SpinMe photographic rotation can cost from as little as £40

As well as clothing, **SpinMe** technology is also ideal for smaller items such as fashion accessories and jewellery.

PREVIOUS   NEXT
CONTACT
QUIT

Examples

www.SpinMe.co.uk

SpinMe

Two fundamental tips for Web words: don't run your text over too great a width or it's very difficult to read – and don't run it on at such length that your reader has to scroll down very far to find out more.

The ideal is to contain everything you need to say within the first screen and then let your reader decide if they want to 'drill down' for further information.

It's not always easy to know how your text is going to appear on every screen since different computers running different programs can display your pages and your text in different ways, but try and get your Web technician to limit the line width.

Above:
An example of writing for a business-to-business digital presentation. SpinMe is a new method of photographing fashion items on live models for improved online display. The copy needed to be informative and persuasive, getting key messages across to those clothing and catalogue companies who are most likely to benefit from these 360 degree photo-rotations.

Client: SpinMe
Copywriter: Rob Bowdery
Art Director: Caroline Walker

Advertising in unusual places △ **Writing to fit**

Can you improve your looks?

An essential consideration for advertising copy is what it looks like on the page, on the billboard, or on the screen. On many occasions we will sacrifice supposedly 'correct' punctuation and even sentence structure to make our messages punchier, shorter and more attractive.

For example, it can look a lot neater to have a headline or subheading that starts with a lower case letter and which doesn't have a full stop at the end. It's more a question of typographical aesthetics rather than literary style; a case of visual appearance over grammatical accuracy.

When it comes to advertising, looks matter since you're trying to attract attention and present your client's product or service in the best possible light.

Similarly, lists do not require a semicolon at the end of every line with a full stop at the end of the final line. It just looks horribly clunky and ugly with so many added dots and squiggles. Leaving out these traditional forms of punctuation makes the text look neater and simpler – and there's no loss of meaning.

Another relatively recent tendency has been to add emphasis to individual words in a heading by increasing their point size in relation to the other words in the line.

Widows are never justified

Some typographical jargon for you there but this stuff is important since the terms 'widow' and 'justification' relate to how your words look on the page. A 'widow' is a word left on its lonesome at the foot of a page or at the end of a paragraph and which therefore sits on its own line in ugly isolation. It looks awkward and is best avoided.

Good typographers will try and sort widows out by adjusting their spacing to take the odd word back or to push another one over to fill out that final line.

Alternatively they will look to you as the writer to make some subtle alterations to change the shape of the copy.

Another typographical consideration is how your words line up on the page. Most text is left-hand 'justified' or lines up neatly on the left-hand side, but it isn't necessary to justify the right-hand edge. In fact it often looks better and proves easier to read if your text isn't justified but left ragged.

Just make sure that your ragged edge has a pleasing shape to it or, again, be prepared to make some copy adjustments to improve its appearance.

does **winter**
make you **feel**
like this?

Above:
Looking good – and I'm not
just talking about the model.
Photographic, typographic,
copywriting and design skills
all combine to make this mailshot
eye-catching and attractive.

Client: Garnier

**Design and typography play a huge
part in the overall effectiveness of
any advert. The best copy in the world
fails to impress if the ad looks dull.**

Advertising in unusual places △ **Writing to fit**

TAIWAN
Delicacy

NETHERLANDS
Delicacy

FRANCE
Delicacy

Never underestimate the importance of local knowledge.

To truly understand a country and its culture, you have to be part of it.

That's why, at HSBC, we have local banks in more countries than anyone else. And all of our offices around the world are staffed by local people.

It's their insight that allows us to recognise financial opportunities invisible to outsiders.

But those opportunities don't just benefit our local customers.

Innovations and ideas are shared throughout the HSBC network, so that everyone who banks with us can benefit.

Think of it as local knowledge that just happens to span the globe.

HSBC
The world's local bank

Issued by HSBC Holdings plc

It appears that English, and in particular American English, has become a world language – or should I say, *lingua franca*, to use that apt old Latin expression? English is now often employed as a common language for business, politics and culture. In fact, there's a general assumption that native speakers of other languages will have at least a basic understanding of English.

However, in practice this is not always the case. And it's a bit arrogant to assume that people of other nations should automatically possess a knowledge of English while many of our own native speakers make little effort to acquire foreign language skills.

On the other hand, it is convenient to speak a language that's attained some form of cultural dominance – even if it does appear primarily due to the power of MTV pop videos.

It's not always easy to come up with the *mot juste* in translation, to tune into the *zeitgeist* and develop a *modus operandi* that covers all continents.

While it might seem quicker and easier to use English for the purpose of marketing to foreign audiences, advertisers need to be aware of the problems they face. The English language will never be universally understood and special allowances must be made for a wide variety of cultural differences.

For example, humour in advertising is popular across the world and yet comedy does not always translate well. For that reason, humour tends to remain within language boundaries – and often within individual nations or specific regions.

Left:
As a bank with a global presence HSBC benefited from a thought-provoking and far-reaching campaign which emphasised local differences rather than pretending that one size fits all in the world of international finance and commerce.

Client: HSBC
Agency: Lowe London

International adverts that have been designed or created to cross country borders can appear bland and superficial because they fail to connect with a particular audience. You can often spot the American or continental TV ad that has been badly dubbed using English voices that don't quite sound right and where the lip movement is out of sync.

And yet there are some companies that succeed in making a virtue out of national differences, either by creating separate ads tailored to the sensibilities of each country or region – or even by highlighting those very differences.

Take the far-reaching HSBC campaign which explained how customs and attitudes vary from country to country. Using the strapline *The world's local bank*, these ads cleverly suggested that they are comfortably *au fait* with local conditions and can therefore help you to do business anywhere in the world.

Whether it's the idea that red is a lucky colour in China but a warning colour in the western world, or it's good manners to finish everything on your plate in European countries but considered a slur on your host's hospitality in the Far East, these ads were both amusing and informative. Above all they emphasised the point that HSBC was a global bank that understood local customs.

Above:
The computer game *Shadow of Rome* was marketed worldwide and so its advertising required translation for foreign audiences, including that of Germany. Here the original headline 'In the arena anything goes' has been adapted to 'Die Spinnen die Romer' which is a phrase made familiar from the German translation of Asterisk the Gaul comic books. And its meaning? 'They're crazy those Romans'.

Client: CAPCOM
Agency: FEREF
Creative and Art Director: Neill Furmston
Copywriter: Amers Sehgal

Advertising around the world

It's fun to be foreign

The technique of using a foreign word or phrase is popular in certain industries, especially in the area of beauty products and perfumes, where French is the favoured language. That's because we tend to think of France, and Paris in particular, as a centre of elegance, fashion and sophistication. A French name has charm, style and a certain *je ne sais quoi, n'est pas?*

Word-check

Vorsprung durch technich – this slightly obscure German phrase was used in the UK to promote Audi cars and yet I don't think many English people could translate their strapline even to this day. But then again, do we *need* to fully understand this line? (Did you spot that split infinitive?) Or is this line just a way of suggesting efficient German engineering: it sounds German and technical, therefore the cars must be well-made.

In fact the line means 'Springing forward through technology', or 'Progress through technology' – although that sounds a bit dull in English, which is presumably why the marketing and advertising people sensibly didn't bother to translate it. *Vorsprung durch technich* appears a lot more dynamic.

Eau de toilette sounds like it would smell so much more pleasant than 'toilet water'. A male fragrance called *Eau Sauvage* seems sexier than *Wild Water* – although, thinking about it, that's not bad and has a butch alliterative quality that might match the underarm deodorant that Burt Reynolds used in *Deliverance*.

Meanwhile 'Rive Gauche' appears more sophisticated, intellectual and Bohemian with its literary and historical associations rather than the flat translation, 'Left Bank'. For the same reason, many fragrances in the UK are labelled 'pour femme' or 'pour homme' just to add a certain French flavour and *cachet* to these products.

Foreign countries are happy to return the favour, using English words and phrases to create their own sense of intrigue and sophistication. And so, to French ears, 'c'est cool' to have a hair extension salon called 'Great Lengths' or to have a selection of engagement rings referred to as 'The bridal collection'.

And, despite some vigorous protests from l'Académie Française about all this creeping 'Franglais', the French still accept English for the international marketing of various beauty items, including a Dior foundation spray called 'Airflash', and l'Oreal hair products called 'Nude Colors'. All these examples of English usage in French ads were gathered from one edition of French *Vogue* magazine.

Writing for foreign markets △ Speaking an international language

If you do have to write an advert or any other marketing copy that you know will need to be translated into other languages, you must try to avoid complex wordplays and local idioms. Otherwise your work might well get lost in translation.

Even countries whose inhabitants often have an excellent command of the English language can miss aspects of English humour. For example, the actor and comedian, Bill Bailey, tells the story of how a great many Norwegians love the TV comedy he appeared in called *Black Books* which is set in a dysfunctional second-hand bookshop run by eccentric Bernard Black, brilliantly played by Dylan Moran.

However, rather than call the show *Black Books* the Norwegians chose to rename this show in a very obvious and un-English way as, *Crazy Shop*. It appears from such small details that we're not always on the same wavelength. No wonder language needs fine-tuning for different audiences.

And if your text can't be translated easily, then it will probably need to be extensively and expensively adapted by a specialist agency. These adaptation agencies tend to employ advertising copywriters who are capable of taking a basic translation and making it work in their own native language. Frequently the adaptations end up being very different from the original text – and for good reason: many clever concepts with witty words don't translate very well.

Take the example of a French airport which wanted to suggest it was the quickest gateway to the skiing resorts in the French Pyrenees. They required their French advert to be adapted into English. The image showed the front of an airplane with ski tips appearing over the cockpit as if they were being carried in the same way as on the roof of a car.

The French headline: *Dans les Pyrenees, la saison commence sur nos pistes* (In the Pyrenees, the season begins on our runways) relies on the fact that the word 'piste' can mean both an airport runway and a ski run. This pun works well in French but it cannot be translated directly into English. An alternative heading was required if the same image of the plane was going to be used.

The English version the adaptation agency came up with relied on a far weaker wordplay: *Skiing in the Pyrenees. There's a way to jet there faster*. My own version, taking on board the comedy visual of the plane carrying skis, also uses a wordplay but one which I hope has greater humorous impact: *Now there's a quicker way to slope off to the Pyrenees*.

Sometimes you have to be brave and tell your client that the same concept is not going to work as well in another language for another culture. It's time to come up with some fresh ideas.

EXCLUSIVEMENT
réservé aux jeunes
forces vives

SFR

Left:
This effective concept for low-price French mobile phone packages used a comic image of a dishevelled young bloke wth the ironic headline 'Exclusivement réservé aux jeunes forces vives' which can be roughly translated as 'Exclusively reserved for dynamic youth' or 'young people with vibrant energy'. Unfortunately these phrases sound awkward in English and yet the original line works extremely well in French. Here's another case where I believe that a different approach would need to be adopted to make this ad work in the UK.

Client: SFR
Agency: Tequila

Some ideas don't travel so well

Just to show that even excellent straplines don't always travel well, there's the story concerning Nike's informal yet motivational line *Just do it*. This line worked well for most of the world but apparently not in France where some people supposedly took it the wrong way and complained. 'I'm not going to *do it* and no one is going to tell me to *do it*!' Perhaps they should have changed it for the French market to *Go your own way* or *Do what you want*.

Word-check

Zeitgeist – there aren't many modern German words that we use in the English language but 'zeitgeist' is a great one and very popular in discussions of marketing as a way of indicating the latest moods and trends. The word translates as 'spirit of the age' (literally 'time-spirit').

Then there's 'schadenfreude' (harm-joy) which is a mean and marvellous term to describe the wicked feeling of pleasure you get from the misfortune of others.

Meanwhile a more pleasant and socially acceptable sensation: that of cosiness and warmth, is suggested by the word 'gemutlicht'. Mmmm nice.

How will you make your mark?

For many years the Spanish tourist board has run a series of full-page ads in weekend colour supplements with the large headline *Spain marks*. To English ears this sounds odd, and no wonder since it appears to be a straight translation from the Spanish, *España te marca* which can be rendered as *Spain marks you* or *Spain leaves its mark on you*, which is already a better expression but still seems a bit peculiar.

The idea of Spain 'leaving its mark' on you when you visit this country and experience its attractions makes a degree of sense but, unfortunately, the word 'mark' retains some negative associations in English. A mark suggests a scar or a bruise, a stain or a dirty mark. Something that leaves its mark is either physically dirty or psychologically damaging, as if you've been marked, or emotionally scarred, for life. (Well, I suppose some holidays can be like that.)

So, as the copywriter, should you try and work with this Spanish phrase or reject the idea entirely and persuade the client to adopt another approach? Here we are in the realm of adaptation rather than mere translation. My recommendation would be to go for a line that reinforces the idea of 'memorable and pleasurable experiences' but which avoids any use of the word 'mark'. But, the choice is yours, since I want you to come up with a suitable alternative. (See 'Now it's your turn'.)

Alternatively, and this can be an effective technique, why not use the original Spanish phrase, 'España te marca', which might well prove charming, evocative and atmospheric? You can then explain the phrase in the body copy and add some examples of the wonderful experiences that might await you. After all, Spanish is the language that's meant to be spoken in Spain, unless you're on the Costa del Fish and Chips.

Above:
Will a holiday in Barcelona
leave its mark on you –
or your clothes? And if it does,
will you be able to wash it out
at low temperatures using
a dermatologically tested,
non-biological washing powder?

Now it's your turn

I haven't offered up my English language
solution to Spain's tourism marketing
conundrum since I thought you might
like to give it a go.

Naturally I didn't want to dismay you with
the sheer excellence of my own offering
(which I am prepared to divulge to readers
in return for a mere £500 paid into
my private Swiss bank account).

In the meantime, it's over to you.
I'm convinced you can come up with
something better than 'Spain marks',
and trust you will enjoy the challenge.

That's the charm and frustration of
copywriting; it's so subjective and there
are no certain solutions – just a series
of alternatives that we have to judge
for their harmony and effectiveness.

Writing for foreign markets △ Speaking an international language △ Lost in translation

Whatever language you're writing in and wherever it has to appear, there's always the danger of embarrassing mistakes when certain words turn out to mean something entirely different in another language.

These errors and oddities can seem very funny to outsiders, especially when the alternative meaning is a rude one or particularly inappropriate, but it can lead to humour-failure among clients and agencies when their advertising campaigns fall flat and expensive revisions are rapidly required.

It's certainly true that some foreign product names really don't travel very well and yet presumably exist quite happily in their native lands. It's that cross-boundary multi-national marketing which can result in some horrible – or amusing – *faux pas*.

For example, Finland has a successful brand of beer with some superb advertising but it's name, *Koff*, suggests to an English audience that it might stick in the throat. Then there's the popular Swedish toffee-filled chocolate bar called *Plopp*, or how about a packet of mixed nuts from the Philippines with the rather charming name, *Ding Dong*? Leslie Phillips would love those.

As I mentioned, it's only when these products travel outside their own territories that they start to sound a bit peculiar or downright odd. And we can certainly return the favour with British names that sound hilariously funny to foreigners.

Right:
Foreign packaging with unusual product names can appear odd or amusing to English eyes and ears. Here are just a few examples.
There's also the tendency for foreign clothing to feature almost random English words and phrases. For this child's casual top, Sportswear has become Sport Swear – although possibly this is an expensive designer label endorsed by Wayne Rooney?

For example, Sean Connery has a surname that wouldn't merit a lifted eyebrow from Roger Moore and yet it sounds very rude and amusing to the French.

Meanwhile, English-speaking brand managers and their naming agencies have got themselves into a pickle over a variety of product names that seemed innocent enough until they fell on foreign ears.

While the word 'mist' in English is an evocative word for low-lying cloud or hazy fog, in German the word means 'manure'. It's therefore no wonder that the launch of a drink called 'Irish Mist' in Germany led to confusion and rather poor sales. It seems that Clairol suffered a similar toe-curling fate when they launched their hair-curling iron 'Mist Stick' on a mystified German market.

You might think you're safe with sets of letters and numbers but when Toyota named their sports car the MR2 they reckoned without French pronunciation. 'M-R-Deux' (or Em-Err-Deux) sounds far too close to 'merde' and so the number '2' was dropped rather hurriedly for the French market before sales went down the toilet.

FOR KIDS
SPORT SWEAR

descends dans la rue pour jouer avec tous tes copains

Rusti Chips
★★★★

SALT

DING
DONG®

mixed
nuts

PASSÉ

PREMIUM QUALITY
TOILET TISSUE

Speaking an international language ▷ Lost in translation

Conclusion

Having trawled through so many aspects of copywriting I suppose I should offer you some concluding words of wisdom. So here goes. Work hard and make your mother proud by becoming a doctor or a lawyer, anything but a copywriter. Well, frankly, I don't need the competition.

But, if you do insist on pursuing this career, try to keep your ideas fresh by working on a wide variety of accounts. Don't get stuck in a rut writing for the same types of product or you could find yourself turning out tired old clichés.

As a copywriter, you might be ghostwriting a chairman's introduction to a firm's official report and accounts in the morning and then creating some sparkling copy for a mailshot aimed at mothers with young children in the afternoon.

The variety is potentially endless which is why, as a copywriter, you must never lose sight of each of the audiences that you're trying to influence. Only then will you be able to keep your ideas and text immediate and relevant.

Remember also that, whatever your profession, we all need to work on our communication skills – whether written or spoken – if we want to get our points across simply and persuasively. Clear and effective communication is at the heart of advertising, preferably all spruced up with wit and style.

And the same principles relate to all forms of communication. The lessons learnt through advertising – keep your message simple and direct; make sure the story you're telling is entertaining and informative – can be applied to so many aspects of business and personal life.

But maybe that's a matter best left to another day. I think I can feel another book coming on...

Recommended reading

Oxford Dictionary of English
Oxford University Press
2nd edition (revised) 2005

Ken Burtenshaw, Nik Mahon
and Caroline Barfoot
**The Fundamentals of
Creative Advertising**
AVA Publishing 2006

Dominic Gettins
The Unwritten Rules of Copywriting
Kogan Page Ltd 2000

The Copy Book
**How 32 of the World's Best
Advertising Writers
Write their Advertising**
D&AD/Rotovision SA 1995

George Felton
Advertising Concept and Copy
WW Norton & Co Inc
2nd edition 2006

Luke Sullivan
**Hey Whipple Squeeze This –
A Guide to Creating Great Ads**
an AdWeek book
published by John Wiley & Sons Inc 1998

Alastair Crompton
The Craft of Copywriting
Century Business Books
1st edition 1979
2nd edition 1987

David Ogilvy
Confessions of an Advertising Man
Longmans Green & Co Ltd
1st published 1963

Alfredo Marcantonio
**Well-written and Red – The Story
of *The Economist* Poster Campaign**
Dakini Books

Bill Bryson
Mother Tongue, The English Language
Penguin Books 1991

Lynne Truss
Eats, Shoots & Leaves
Profile Books 2003

Rosie Walford
**Shelf Life, A Celebration of the
World's Quirkiest Brands**
Bloomsbury Publishing 2004

This is hardly a comprehensive list but here are a few terms that you're likely to come across in the world of advertising and copywriting – some of which I've explained in the text but here's a reminder anyway.

Account ► each client company, organisation – or even individual brand – that an agency or consultancy works on is called an 'account', hence 'account handlers', 'account directors', 'account managers', etc.

Apostrophe ► that tricky little symbol that so many people don't quite know where to stick, despite the efforts of their English language teachers. (Turn to page 76 for a detailed explanation that could save your future blushes.)

Art Director ► a posh title for the senior designers who work at an ad agency (as distinct at times from mere artworkers) and, if copywriters weren't such nice people, a potential cause for resentment since we're not called 'Copy Directors'.

Artworker ► slightly patronising term for someone who puts final artwork together. Artworkers need to have excellent Mac skills and a profound knowledge of layout and typography, etc. The best artworkers can take a skimpy scamp and turn it into a powerful advert.

Body copy ► the main text of an advert or other promotional item and, typically, the longer copy that appears below the headline.

Brief ► this written document doesn't have to be very brief but it does help if the description of the task in hand is kept short and relevant, containing all the details required by the creative team to get their thinking juices flowing. We need to know all about the product or service being advertised; the target audience for our communication; ideally the media in which our advertising is to appear, and what this advertising is intended to achieve. Without such clear objectives, even the best creatives are likely to flounder.

Copy ► the words that are written for adverts, brochures, newspapers and magazines, etc. (Although you're not meant to simply copy them from someone else! That's cheating. However, in the world of advertising, 'borrowing' good ideas is standard practice.)

Copyright ► sometimes confused with 'copywriting', but this is a legal term which refers to the intellectual property rights of any such item as a novel, a design, or a product, etc. and therefore who is entitled to royalty payments when such an item is copied or reproduced.

Copywriter ► a harmless drudge who is generally poorly rewarded for generating scintillating ideas and sparkling text.

Creatives ► a rather grand and flattering term for the art directors and copywriters who put their heads together to come up with creative concepts.

Mac ▶ Apple Macintoshes – or Apple Macs – have become the standard computer system in use in advertising agencies and design consultancies, primarily because the platform they operate on was, in the 1980s, the first to support efficient design packages such as PageMaker, Illustrator, Quark XPress, FreeHand and Photoshop.

Planners ▶ as a relatively recent phenomenon in the ad agency, planners fulfil a role that was usually the responsibility of busy account handlers, which is to acquire as much information about the project in hand, develop effective advertising strategies and then convey that information to the creative team. (Not to be confused with media planners, who are responsible for sourcing and negotiating cost-effective media placement, eg buying ad space in newspapers, on billboards and online, etc.)

Scamps ▶ a rather cute term for a roughly drawn visual, also called a 'rough'. Formerly scamps were always hand-drawn using marker pens and that look is coming back into favour, although many 'scamped up' ideas are now produced on the Mac giving them a more finished look that can be very close to finished artwork.

Straplines ▶ a short slogan that aims to sum up a business, product or brand in a memorable and consistent way. Often appears next to or near the company logo to reinforce the brand image, eg *Go to work on an egg*; *Try something new today*, etc.

Suits ▶ comical and slightly derogatory term for account handlers due to their supposedly more formal dress sense since they have to meet with clients and need to present a smarter appearance than that of the artfully dishevelled 'creatives'.

Target audience ▶ a critical element in all marketing and advertising activities since we have to know who we're trying to target with our promotional messages. However, it's best not to think of these people as an attentive audience who have paid good money to get into some metaphorical theatre to watch your ad! You're going to have to work hard to grab and keep their attention.

Tone of voice ▶ well, self-evident really! It really does help if you are able to write in a wide variety of styles so you can appeal to many and various target audiences. Each ad you write is likely to be angled at a different audience so you have to talk the language they will understand – and respond positively towards.

USP ▶ a unique selling point or proposition. As mentioned on page 38, not all USPs are unique so it can be a bit of a misleading statement. It's great if the item you're being asked to advertise has a distinct and unique advantage over competitors' similar products but often we'll settle for what appears to be a single strong selling proposition and hang our benefit-led advertising on that hook.

Acknowledgements and credits

With thanks to...

In addition to thanking the many advertising folk who have lent me some of their best work and who are credited in the preceding pages, I'd like to single out for further praise the following people:

Lucy Tipton of AVA Publishing – who performed the role of nagging editor with wit and charm – and who only took out a few of my best jokes.

Leafy Robinson of AVA Publishing – who picked up on Lucy's work in the closing stages while her colleague finally got round to getting married.

With great thanks to David Shaw for all his hard work and aesthetic tinkering to make the book look so good.

Thanks also to:

Brian Morris, Sanaz Nazemi and Renee Last at AVA Publishing.

Adrian Crane of Factor 3 for his help and support. An excellent conceptual copywriter whose modesty puts many creatives to shame.

Amers Sehgal of More Design – thanks for your enthusiasm and sorting out some excellent advertising examples, including some of your own.

Adrian Brown of FEREF – for organising and supplying hi-res imagery for the book.

Maya Rowson – for her unfailing support and the loan of her portfolio.

Charlotte Ward Kidner – for our long-term association on so many design projects.

Fran Caplan of McCann-Erickson

Joslyn Tinker and Hannah Leathers of Lowe London

Dan Worrell of Karmarama

Chika Ochonogor of Unilever

Nick Thomas of Target Direct

Nick Holmes of Different Kettle

Philip Hickes of Golley Slater, Cardiff

Nigel Clifton of EHS Brann, London

Frazer Howard of EHS Brann, Cirencester

Jon Dobinson of Phosphorus

Selina Gladstone-Thompson of Publicis

Nick Ting of TBWA

Antoinette De Lisser of Beattie McGuinness Bungay

Richard Wood, Chris Purnell and Alec Stoat at Bovis Homes

Linda Johnston at The Fitness Team

Sharon Graves at Spirax Sarco

Cathy Hawkins, National Membership Development Manager, English Heritage

David Cook, ace photographer, for shooting fish in his bath, and Ian 'Jake' Jakeway for dressing up in rubber – not that he needs much persuading.

John Moore for taking so many of the photos for the book, including the front cover shot.

Thanks also to baby Leo Smith and his parents, Franki and Mat – photographed by John Moore of Two Front Teeth.

Ed Swarbrick and his daughter Zosia and son William for providing suitable Spanish souvenirs.

Christopher Knowles for a final image.

And finally, my wife Rachel for offering to proofread – despite not liking me working for so long and so late on this book.